LEWISHAM PUBLIC LIBRARIES

Hours: 10 a.m. - 7-30 p.m. (Saturdays 10 a.m. - 6 p.m.), excepting Christmas Day, Good Friday, Easter Saturday and Bank Holidays.

Renewable by phone, letter or personal call unless required by another reader.

EDINBURGH

The New Town from the Calton Hill.

EDINBURGH

Picturesque Notes

by

Robert Louis Stevenson

WITH ILLUSTRATIONS

BY

T. HAMILTON CRAWFORD

Member of the Royal Scottish Water Colour Society

LONDON

SEELEY AND CO. LIMITED

38 GREAT RUSSELL STREET

1900

CONTENTS

CHAPTER VIII.

CHAPTER IX.

CHAPTER X.

LIST OF ILLUSTRATIONS

PLATES

ILLUSTRATIONS IN THE TEXT

EDINBURGH

CHAPTER I

INTRODUCTORY

THE ancient and famous metropolis of the North sits overlooking a windy estuary from the slope and summit of three hills. No situation could be more commanding for the head city of a kingdom; none better chosen for noble prospects. From her tall precipice and terraced gardens she looks far and wide on the sea and broad champaigns. To the east you may catch at sunset the spark of the May lighthouse, where the Firth expands into the German Ocean; and away to the west, over all the carse of Stirling, you can see the first snows upon Ben Ledi.

B

But Edinburgh pays cruelly for her high
seat in one of the vilest climates under heaven.
She is liable to be beaten upon by all the
winds that blow, to be drenched with rain, to
be buried in cold sea fogs out of the east, and
powdered with the snow as it comes flying
southward from the Highland hills. The
weather is raw and boisterous in winter, shifty
and ungenial in summer, and a downright
meteorological purgatory in the spring. The
delicate die early, and I, as a survivor, among
bleak winds and plumping rain, have been
sometimes tempted to envy them their fate.
For all who love shelter and the blessings
of the sun, who hate dark weather and per-
petual tilting against squalls, there could
scarcely be found a more unhomely and
harassing place of residence. Many such
aspire angrily after that Somewhere-else of
the imagination, where all troubles are supposed to end. They lean over the great bridge
which joins the New Town with the Old—

that windiest spot, or high altar, in this
northern temple of the winds—and watch

On the
NORTH
BRIDGE

the trains smoking out from under them and
vanishing into the tunnel on a voyage to
brighter skies. Happy the passengers who

shake off the dust of Edinburgh, and have heard for the last time the cry of the east wind among her chimney-tops! And yet the place establishes an interest in people's hearts; go where they will, they find no

Holyrood
Palace

city of the same distinction; go where they will, they take a pride in their old home.

Venice, it has been said, differs from all other cities in the sentiment which she inspires. The rest may have admirers; she only, a famous fair one, counts lovers in her train. And indeed, even by her kindest friends, Edinburgh is not considered in a similar sense. These like her for many reasons, not any one of which is satisfactory in itself. They like her whimsically, if you will, and somewhat as a virtuoso dotes upon his cabinet. Her attraction is romantic in the narrowest meaning of the term. Beautiful as she is, she is not so much beautiful as interesting. She is pre-eminently Gothic, and all the more so since she has set herself off with some Greek airs, and erected classic temples on her crags. In a word, and above all, she is a curiosity. The Palace of Holyrood has been left aside in the growth of Edinburgh, and stands grey and silent in a workmen's quarter and among breweries and gas works. It is a house of many memories. Great people of yore, kings and queens, buffoons and grave ambassadors, played their stately farce for centuries in Holyrood. Wars

have been plotted, dancing has lasted deep
into the night, murder has been done in its

Prince Charlie at Holyrood

chambers. There Prince Charlie held his
phantom *levées,* and in a very gallant manner
represented a fallen dynasty for some hours.

The Lord Commissioner's Levée

Now, all these things of clay are mingled with the dust, the king's crown itself is shown for sixpence to the vulgar; but the stone palace has outlived these changes. For fifty weeks together, it is no more than a show for tourists and a museum of old furniture; but on the fifty-first, behold the palace re-awakened and mimicking its past. The Lord Commissioner, a kind of stage sovereign, sits among stage courtiers ; a coach and six and clattering escort come and go before the gate ; at night, the windows are lighted up, and its near neighbours, the workmen, may dance in their own houses to the palace music. And in this the palace is typical. There is a spark among the embers ; from time to time the old volcano smokes. Edinburgh has but partly abdicated, and still wears, in parody, her metropolitan trappings. Half a capital and half a country town, the whole city leads a double existence ; it has long trances of the one and flashes of the other ; like the king of the Black

Isles, it is half alive and half a monumental marble. There are armed men and cannon in the citadel overhead ; you may see the troops marshalled on the high parade ; and at night

The Argyle Battery

after the early winter evenfall, and in the morning before the laggard winter dawn, the wind carries abroad over Edinburgh the sound of drums and bugles. Grave judges sit bewigged in what was once the scene of imperial

"A Royal Proclamation

deliberations. Close by in the High Street
perhaps the trumpets may sound about the

stroke of noon ; and you see a troop of citizens in tawdry masquerade ; tabard above, heather-mixture trouser below, and the men themselves trudging in the mud among unsympathetic bystanders. The grooms of a well-appointed circus tread the streets with a better presence. And yet these are the Heralds and Pursuivants of Scotland, who are about to proclaim a new law of the United Kingdom before two-score boys, and thieves, and hackney-coachmen. Meanwhile every hour the bell of the University rings out over the hum of the streets, and every hour a double tide of students, coming and going, fills the deep archways. And lastly, one night in the springtime—or say one morning rather, at the peep of day—late folk may hear the voices of many men singing a psalm in unison from a church on one side of the old High Street ; and a little after, or perhaps a little before, the sound of many men singing a psalm in unison from another church on the opposite side of the

ACADEMIA · IACOBI · VI · NATVM
ANNO · POST · CHRISTVM · NATVM
M D C L X X I I · RENOVATVM · ELD
ANNOQVE · GEORGII · III · MAG · BRITANNIÆ
REGNANTE · GEORGIO · III · PRÆFECTVS · ROBERTSON
REGNANTE · EDINBVRGI · ARIO · HELMO · ROBERTSON
ACADEMIÆ · VMARIO · RO · R TO · ADAM ·

The UNIVERSITY

way. There will be something in the words
about the dew of Hermon, and how goodly it
is to see brethren dwelling together in unity.
And the late folk will tell themselves that all
this singing denotes the conclusion of two yearly
ecclesiastical parliaments—the parliaments of
Churches which are brothers in many admirable
virtues, but not specially like brothers in this
particular of a tolerant and peaceful life.

Again, meditative people will find a charm
in a certain consonancy between the aspect
of the city and its odd and stirring history.
Few places, if any, offer a more barbaric
display of contrasts to the eye. In the very
midst stands one of the most satisfactory
crags in nature—a Bass Rock upon dry land,
rooted in a garden, shaken by passing trains,
carrying a crown of battlements and turrets,
and describing its warlike shadow over the
liveliest and brightest thoroughfare of the
New Town. From their smoky beehives,
ten stories high, the unwashed look down

upon the open squares and gardens of the wealthy; and gay people sunning themselves along Princes Street, with its mile of commercial palaces all beflagged upon some great occasion, see, across a gardened valley set with statues, where the washings of the Old Town flutter in the breeze at its high windows. And then, upon all sides, what a clashing of architecture! In this one valley, where the life of the town goes most busily forward, there may be seen, shown one above and behind another by the accidents of the ground, buildings in almost every style upon the globe. Egyptian and Greek temples, Venetian palaces and Gothic spires, are huddled one over another in a most admired disorder; while, above all, the brute mass of the Castle and the summit of Arthur's Seat look down upon these imitations with a becoming dignity, as the works of Nature may look down upon the monuments of Art. But Nature is a more indiscriminate patroness than we imagine, and in no way frightened of a strong effect. The birds roost as willingly among the Corin-

The
Royal Institution
and
National Gallery

thian capitals as in the crannies of the crag; the same atmosphere and daylight clothe the eternal rock and yesterday's imitation portico;

C

and as the soft northern sunshine throws out everything into a glorified distinctness—or easterly mists, coming up with the blue evening, fuse all these incongruous features

The Old Town from the New

into one, and the lamps begin to glitter along the street, and faint lights to burn in the high windows across the valley—the feeling grows upon you that this also is a piece of nature in the most intimate sense; that this profusion of eccentricities, this dream in masonry and living rock, is not a drop-scene in a theatre, but a city in the world of every-day reality, connected by railway and telegraph-wire with all the capitals of Europe, and inhabited by citizens of the familiar type, who keep ledgers, and attend church, and have sold their immortal portion to a daily paper. By all the canons of romance, the place demands to be half deserted and leaning towards decay; birds we might admit in profusion, the play of the sun and winds, and a few gipsies encamped in the chief thoroughfare; but these citizens, with their cabs and tramways, their trains and posters, are altogether out of key. Chartered tourists, they make free with historic localities, and rear their young among the most picturesque sites with a grand human indifference. To see them thronging by, in their neat clothes and conscious moral rectitude, and with a little air

of possession that verges on the absurd, is
not the least striking feature of the place.*

And the story of the town is as eccentric as
its appearance. For centuries it was a capital
thatched with heather, and more than once,
in the evil days of English invasion, it has
gone up in flame to heaven, a beacon to ships

---

* These sentences have, I hear, given offence in my
native town, and a proportionable pleasure to our rivals of
Glasgow. I confess the news caused me both pain and
merriment. May I remark, as a balm for wounded fellow-
townsmen, that there is nothing deadly in my accusations ?
Small blame to them if they keep ledgers : 'tis an excellent
business habit. Churchgoing is not, that ever I heard, a
subject of reproach ; decency of linen is a mark of pros-
perous affairs, and conscious moral rectitude one of the
tokens of good living. It is not their fault if the city calls
for something more specious by way of inhabitants. A man
in a frock-coat looks out of place upon an Alp or Pyramid,
although he has the virtues of a Peabody and the talents of
a Bentham. And let them console themselves—they do as
well as anybody else ; the population of (let us say) Chicago
would cut quite as rueful a figure on the same romantic
stage. To the Glasgow people I would say only one word,
but that is of gold : *I have not yet written a book about
Glasgow.*

at sea. It was the jousting-ground of jealous
nobles, not only on Greenside or by the King's
Stables, where set tournaments were fought

*Shops by
St. Giles's*

to the sound of trumpets and under the
authority of the royal presence, but in every
alley where there was room to cross swords,
and in the main street, where popular tumult

under the Blue Blanket alternated with the brawls of outlandish clansmen and retainers. Down in the palace John Knox reproved his queen in the accents of modern democracy. In the town, in one of those little shops plastered like so many swallows' nests among the buttresses of the old Cathedral, that familiar autocrat, James VI., would gladly share a bottle of wine with George Heriot the goldsmith. Up on the Pentland Hills, that so quietly look down on the Castle with the city lying in waves around it, those mad and dismal fanatics, the Sweet Singers, haggard from long exposure on the moors, sat day and night with 'tearful psalms' to see Edinburgh consumed with fire from heaven, like another Sodom or Gomorrah. There, in the Grass-market, stiff-necked, covenanting heroes, offered up the often unnecessary, but not less honourable, sacrifice of their lives, and bade eloquent farewell to sun, moon, and stars, and earthly friendships, or died silent to the roll

© JTB

of drums. Down by yon outlet rode Gra-
hame of Claverhouse and his thirty dragoons,
with the town beating to arms behind their
horses' tails—a sorry handful thus riding for
their lives, but with a man at the head who
was to return in a different temper, make a
dash that staggered Scotland to the heart, and
die happily in the thick of fight. There
Aikenhead was hanged for a piece of boyish
incredulity ; there, a few years afterwards,
David Hume ruined Philosophy and Faith,
an undisturbed and well-reputed citizen ; and
thither, in yet a few years more, Burns came
from the plough-tail, as to an academy of
gilt unbelief and artificial letters. There,
when the great exodus was made across the
valley, and the New Town began to spread
abroad its draughty parallelograms and rear
its long frontage on the opposing hill, there
was such a flitting, such a change of domicile
and dweller, as was never excelled in the
history of cities : the cobbler succeeded the

earl; the beggar ensconced himself by the judge's chimney; what had been a palace was used as a pauper refuge; and great mansions were so parcelled out among the least and lowest in society, that the hearthstone of the old proprietor was thought large enough to be partitioned off into a bedroom by the new.

of drums. Down by yon outlet rode Gra-
hame of Claverhouse and his thirty dragoons,
with the town beating to arms behind their
horses' tails—a sorry handful thus riding for
their lives, but with a man at the head who
was to return in a different temper, make a
dash that staggered Scotland to the heart, and
die happily in the thick of fight. There
Aikenhead was hanged for a piece of boyish
incredulity ; there, a few years afterwards,
David Hume ruined Philosophy and Faith,
an undisturbed and well-reputed citizen ; and
thither, in yet a few years more, Burns came
from the plough-tail, as to an academy of
gilt unbelief and artificial letters. There,
when the great exodus was made across the
valley, and the New Town began to spread
abroad its draughty parallelograms and rear
its long frontage on the opposing hill, there
was such a flitting, such a change of domicile
and dweller, as was never excelled in the
history of cities : the cobbler succeeded the

earl; the beggar ensconced himself by the judge's chimney; what had been a palace was used as a pauper refuge; and great mansions were so parcelled out among the least and lowest in society, that the hearthstone of the old proprietor was thought large enough to be partitioned off into a bedroom by the new.

CHAPTER II

THE Old Town, it is pretended, is the chief characteristic, and, from a picturesque point of view, the liver-wing of Edinburgh. It is one of the most common forms of depreciation to throw cold water on the whole by adroit over-commendation of a part, since everything worth judging, whether it be a man, a work of art, or only a fine city, must be judged upon its merits as a whole. The Old Town depends for much of its effect on the new quarters that lie around it, on the sufficiency of its situation, and on the hills that back it up. If you were to set it somewhere else by itself,

it would look remarkably like Stirling in a
bolder and loftier edition. The point is to
see this embellished Stirling planted in the
midst of a large, active, and fantastic modern
city ; for there the two re-act in a picturesque
sense, and the one is the making of the
other.

The Old Town occupies a sloping ridge
or tail of diluvial matter, protected, in some
subsidence of the waters, by the Castle cliffs
which fortify it to the west. On the one
side of it and the other the new towns of the
south and of the north occupy their lower,
broader, and more gentle hill-tops. Thus,
the quarter of the Castle overtops the whole
city and keeps an open view to sea and land.
It dominates for miles on every side ; and
people on the decks of ships, or ploughing
in quiet country places over in Fife, can see
the banner on the Castle battlements, and
the smoke of the Old Town blowing abroad
over the subjacent country. A city that is

The City from Salisbury Crags.

T. H. CRAWFORD

set upon a hill. It was, I suppose, from this
distant aspect that she got her nickname of
Auld Reekie. Perhaps it was given her by
people who had never crossed her doors : day
after day, from their various rustic Pisgahs,
they had seen the pile of building on the
hill-top, and the long plume of smoke over
the plain ; so it appeared to them ; so it had
appeared to their fathers tilling the same field ;
and as that was all they knew of the place,
it could be all expressed in these two words.

Indeed, even on a nearer view, the Old
Town is properly smoked ; and though it is
well washed with rain all the year round, it
has a grim and sooty aspect among its younger
suburbs. It grew, under the law that regu-
lates the growth of walled cities in precarious
situations, not in extent, but in height and
density. Public buildings were forced,
wherever there was room for them, into the
midst of thoroughfares ; thoroughfares were
diminished into lanes ; houses sprang up story

after story, neighbour mounting upon neighbour's shoulder, as in some Black Hole of Calcutta, until the population slept fourteen or fifteen deep in a vertical direction. The tallest of these *lands*, as they are locally termed, have long since been burnt out; but to this day it is not uncommon to see eight or ten windows at a flight; and the cliff of building which hangs imminent over Waverley Bridge would still put many natural precipices to shame. The cellars are already high above the gazer's head, planted on the steep hillside; as for the garret, all the furniture may be in the pawnshop, but it commands a famous prospect to the Highland hills. The poor man may roost up there in the centre of Edinburgh, and yet have a peep of the green country from his window; he shall see the quarters of the well-to-do fathoms underneath, with their broad squares and gardens; he shall have nothing overhead but a few spires, the stone top-gallants of the city;

WARRISTON'S CLOSE

MACLAREN S...

*Warriston's
Close*

and perhaps the wind may reach him with a
rustic pureness, and bring a smack of the sea,
or of flowering lilacs in the spring.

It is almost the correct literary sentiment
to deplore the revolutionary improvements
of Mr. Chambers and his following. It is
easy to be a conservator of the discomforts
of others ; indeed, it is only our good qualities
we find it irksome to conserve. Assuredly, in
driving streets through the black labyrinth, a
few curious old corners have been swept away,
and some associations turned out of house and
home. But what slices of sunlight, what
breaths of clean air, have been let in ! And
what a picturesque world remains untouched !
You go under dark arches, and down dark
stairs and alleys. The way is so narrow that
you can lay a hand on either wall ; so steep
that, in greasy winter weather, the pavement
is almost as treacherous as ice. Washing
dangles above washing from the windows ;
the houses bulge outwards upon flimsy

brackets ; you see a bit of sculpture in a dark
corner ; at the top of all, a gable and a few
crowsteps are printed on the sky.   Here, you

THE
OLD
WHITE HORSE
INN,
CANONGATE

come into a court where the children are at
play and the grown people sit upon their doorsteps, and perhaps a church spire shows itself
above the roofs.   Here, in the narrowest of

*High Street
at the Cross Well*

the entry, you find a great old mansion still erect, with some insignia of its former state—

Doorhead in the Canongate

some scutcheon, some holy or courageous motto, on the lintel. The local antiquary points out where famous and well-born people

had their lodging; and as you look up, out
pops the head of a slatternly woman from the
countess's window.   The Bedouins camp

Doorhead in Candlemakers' Row

within Pharaoh's palace walls, and the old
war-ship is given over to the rats.   We are
already a far way from the days when
powdered heads were plentiful in these alleys,

with jolly, port-wine faces underneath. Even
in the chief thoroughfares Irish washings

Doorhead in Lady Stair's Close

flutter at the windows, and the pavements are
encumbered with loiterers.

These loiterers are a true character of the
scene. Some shrewd Scotch workmen may
have paused on their way to a job, debating

Church affairs and politics with their tools upon their arm. But the most part are of a different order—skulking jail-birds ; unkempt, bare-foot children ; big-mouthed, robust women, in a sort of uniform of striped flannel petticoat and short tartan shawl : among these, a few supervising constables and a dismal sprinkling of mutineers and broken men from higher ranks in society, with some mark of better days upon them, like a brand. In a place no larger than Edinburgh, and where the traffic is mostly centred in five or six chief streets, the same face comes often under the notice of an idle stroller. In fact, from this point of view, Edinburgh is not so much a small city as the largest of small towns. It is scarce possible to avoid observing your neighbours ; and I never yet heard of any one who tried. It has been my fortune, in this anonymous accidental way, to watch more than one of these downward travellers for some stages on the

road to ruin. One man must have been

The Canongate Cross

upwards of sixty before I first observed him, and he made then a decent, personable figure in broadcloth of the best. For three years he kept falling—grease coming and buttons going from the square-skirted coat, the face puffing and pimpling, the shoulders growing bowed, the hair falling scant and grey upon his head ; and the last that ever I saw of him, he was standing at the mouth of an entry with several men in moleskin, three parts drunk, and his old black raiment daubed with mud. I fancy that I still can hear him laugh. There was something heart-breaking in this gradual de-clension at so advanced an age ; you would have thought a man of sixty out of the reach of these calamities ; you would have thought that he was niched by that time into a safe place in life, whence he could pass quietly and honourably into the grave.

One of the earliest marks of these *dégrin-golades* is, that the victim begins to disappear from the New Town thoroughfares, and takes to the High Street, like a wounded animal to the woods. And such an one is the type of

A Dégringolade

the quarter. It also has fallen socially. A scutcheon over the door somewhat jars in sentiment where there is a washing at every window. The old man, when I saw him last, wore the coat in which he had played the gentleman three years before ; and that was just what gave him so pre-eminent an air of wretchedness.

It is true that the over-population was at least as dense in the epoch of lords and ladies, and that now-a-days some customs which made Edinburgh notorious of yore have been fortunately pretermitted. But an aggregation of comfort is not distasteful like an aggregation of the reverse. Nobody cares how many lords and ladies, and divines and lawyers, may have been crowded into these houses in the past —perhaps the more the merrier. The glasses clink around the china punch-bowl, some one touches the virginals, there are peacocks' feathers on the chimney, and the tapers burn clear and pale in the red firelight. That is not an ugly picture in itself, nor will it become ugly upon repetition. All the better if the like were going on in every second room; the *land* would only look the more inviting. Times are changed. In one house, perhaps, twoscore families herd together ; and, perhaps, not one of them is wholly out of the reach of want. The great hotel is given over to discomfort from the foundation to the chimney-tops ; everywhere a pinching, narrow habit, scanty meals, and an air of sluttishness and dirt. In the first room there is a birth, in another a death, in a third a sordid drinking-bout, and the detective and the Bible-reader cross upon the stairs. High words are audible from dwelling to dwelling, and children have a strange experience from the first ; only a robust soul, you would think, could grow up in such conditions without hurt. And even if God tempers His dispensations to the young, and all the ill does not arise that our apprehensions may forecast, the sight of such a way of

Former Inhabitants of the High Street

living is disquieting to people who are more happily circumstanced. Social inequality is

The Cowgate from the South Bridge

nowhere more ostentatious than at Edinburgh.

I have mentioned already how, to the stroller along Princes Street, the High Street callously exhibits its back garrets. It is true, there is a garden between. And although nothing could be more glaring by way of contrast, sometimes the opposition is more immediate ; sometimes the thing lies in a nutshell, and there is not so much as a blade of grass between the rich and poor. To look over the South Bridge and see the Cowgate below full of crying hawkers, is to view one rank of society from another in the twinkling of an eye.

One night I went along the Cowgate after every one was a-bed but the policeman, and stopped by hazard before a tall *land*. The moon touched upon its chimneys, and shone blankly on the upper windows ; there was no light anywhere in the great bulk of building ; but as I stood there it seemed to me that I could hear quite a body of quiet sounds from the interior ; doubtless there were many clocks ticking, and people snoring on their backs.

And thus, as I fancied, the dense life within made itself faintly audible in my ears, family after family contributing its quota to the general hum, and the whole pile beating in tune to its timepieces, like a great disordered heart. Perhaps it was little more than a fancy altogether, but it was strangely impressive at the time, and gave me an imaginative measure of the disproportion between the quantity of living flesh and the trifling walls that separated and contained it.

There was nothing fanciful, at least, but every circumstance of terror and reality, in the fall of the *land* in the High Street. The build-ing had grown rotten to the core; the entry underneath had suddenly closed up so that the scavenger's barrow could not pass; cracks and reverberations sounded through the house at night; the inhabitants of the huge old human bee-hive discussed their peril when they en-countered on the stair; some had even left their dwellings in a panic of fear, and returned

E 2

to them again in a fit of economy or self-respect; when, in the black hours of a Sunday morning, the whole structure ran together with a hideous uproar and tumbled story upon story to the ground. The physical shock was felt far and near; and the moral shock travelled with the morning milkmaid into all the suburbs. The church-bells never sounded more dismally over Edinburgh than that grey forenoon. Death had made a brave harvest; and, like Samson, by pulling down one roof destroyed many a home. None who saw it can have forgotten the aspect of the gable : here it was plastered, there papered, according to the rooms; here the kettle still stood on the hob, high overhead; and there a cheap picture of the Queen was pasted over the chimney. So, by this disaster, you had a glimpse into the life of thirty families, all suddenly cut off from the revolving years. The *land* had fallen ; and with the *land* how much ! Far in the country, people saw a gap in the city ranks, and the sun looked through between the chimneys in an unwonted place. And all over the world, in London, in Canada, in New Zealand, fancy what a multitude of people could exclaim with truth : ' The house that I was born in fell last night ! '

CHAPTER III

TIME has wrought its changes most notably around the precinct of St. Giles's Church. The church itself, if it were not for the spire, would be unrecognisable; the *Krames* are all gone, not a shop is left to shelter in its buttresses ; and zealous magistrates and a misguided architect have shorn the design of manhood, and left it poor, naked, and pitifully pretentious. As St. Giles's must have had in former days a rich and quaint appearance now forgotten, so the neighbourhood was bustling, sunless, and romantic. It was here that the town was most overbuilt ; but the overbuilding has been all rooted out, and not only a free fair-

T. M. CRAWFORD. R.S.W.

way left along the High Street with an open
space on either side of the church, but a great
porthole, knocked in the main line of the *lands*,
gives an outlook to the north and the New
Town.

There is a silly story of a subterranean passage between the Castle and Holyrood, and a
bold Highland piper who volunteered to ex-
plore its windings. He made his entrance by
the upper end, playing a strathspey; the curious
footed it after him down the street, following
his descent by the sound of the chanter from
below; until all of a sudden, about the level of
St. Giles's, the music came abruptly to an end,
and the people in the street stood at fault with
hands uplifted. Whether he was choked with
gases, or perished in a quag, or was removed
bodily by the Evil One, remains a point of
doubt; but the piper has never again been seen
or heard of from that day to this. Perhaps he
wandered down into the land of Thomas the
Rhymer, and some day, when it is least ex-

pected, may take a thought to revisit the sunlit upper world. That will be a strange moment for the cabmen on the stance besides St. Giles's, when they hear the drone of his pipes re-ascending from the bowels of the earth below their horses' feet.

But it is not only pipers who have vanished, many a solid bulk of masonry has been likewise spirited into the air. Here, for example, is the shape of a heart let into the causeway. This was the site of the Tolbooth, the Heart of Midlothian, a place old in story and namefather to a noble book. The walls are now down in the dust; there is no more *squalor carceris* for merry debtors, no more cage for the old, ac-knowledged prison-breaker; but the sun and the wind play freely over the foundations of the jail. Nor is this the only memorial that the pavement keeps of former days. The ancient burying-ground of Edinburgh lay be-hind St. Giles's Church, running downhill to the Cowgate and covering the site of the pres-

ent Parliament House. It has disappeared as
utterly as the prison or the Luckenbooths ; and

JOHN
KNOX'S
STUDY

for those ignorant of its history, I know only
one token that remains. In the Parliament
Close, trodden daily underfoot by advocates,
two letters and a date mark the resting-place of

the man who made Scotland over again in his
own image, the indefatigable, undissuadable
John Knox. He sleeps within call of the
church that so often echoed to his preaching.

Hard by the reformer, a bandy-legged and
garlanded Charles Second, made of lead, be-
strides a tun-bellied charger. The King has his
back turned, and, as you look, seems to be
trotting clumsily away from such a dangerous
neighbour. Often, for hours together, these
two will be alone in the Close, for it lies out of
the way of all but legal traffic. On one side
the south wall of the church, on the other the
arcades of the Parliament House, inclose this
irregular bight of causeway and describe their
shadows on it in the sun. At either end, from
round St. Giles's buttresses, you command a
look into the High Street with its motley passengers ; but the stream goes by, east and west,
and leaves the Parliament Close to Charles the
Second and the birds. Once in a while, a patient crowd may be seen loitering there all day,

some eating fruit, some reading a newspaper ; and to judge by their quiet demeanour, you would think they were waiting for a distribution of soup-tickets. The fact is far otherwise ; within in the Justiciary Court a man is upon trial for his life, and these are some of the curious for whom the gallery was found too narrow. Towards afternoon, if the prisoner is unpopular, there will be a round of hisses when he is brought forth. Once in a while, too, an advocate in wig and gown, hand upon mouth, full of pregnant nods, sweeps to and fro in the arcade listening to an agent ; and at certain regular hours a whole tide of lawyers hurries across the space.

The Parliament Close has been the scene of marking incidents in Scottish history. Thus, when the Bishops were ejected from the Convention in 1688, ' all fourteen of them gathered together with pale faces and stood in a cloud in the Parliament Close : ' poor episcopal personages who were done with fair weather for life !

Some of the west-country Societarians standing
by, who would have 'rejoiced more than in
great sums' to be at their hanging, hustled
them so rudely that they knocked their heads
together. It was not magnanimous behaviour
to dethroned enemies ; but one, at least, of the
Societarians had groaned in the *boots*, and they
had all seen their dear friends upon the scaffold.
Again, at the ' woeful Union,' it was here that
people crowded to escort their favourite from
the last of Scottish parliaments : people flushed
with nationality, as Boswell would have said,
ready for riotous acts, and fresh from throwing
stones at the author of ' Robinson Crusoe ' as he
looked out of window.

One of the pious in the seventeenth century,
going to pass his *trials* (examinations as we now
say) for the Scottish Bar, beheld the Parliament
Close open and had a vision of the mouth of
Hell. This, and small wonder, was the means
of his conversion. Nor was the vision unsuitable to the locality ; for after an hospital, what

Advocate and Agent

uglier piece is there in civilisation than a court of law? Hither come envy, malice, and all uncharitableness to wrestle it out in public tourney; crimes, broken fortunes, severed households, the knave and his victim, gravitate to this low building with the arcade. To how many has not St. Giles's bell told the first hour after ruin? I think I see them pause to count the strokes, and wander on again into the moving High Street, stunned and sick at heart.

A pair of swing doors gives admittance to a hall with a carved roof, hung with legal portraits, adorned with legal statuary, lighted by windows of painted glass, and warmed by three vast fires. This is the *Salle des pas perdus* of the Scottish Bar. Here, by a ferocious custom, idle youths must promenade from ten till two. From end to end, singly or in pairs or trios, the gowns and wigs go back and forward. Through a hum of talk and footfalls, the piping tones of a Macer announce a fresh cause and call upon

the names of those concerned. Intelligent men
have been walking here daily for ten or twenty
years without a rag of business or a shilling of
reward. In process of time, they may perhaps
be made the Sheriff-Substitute and Fountain of
Justice at Lerwick or Tobermory. There is
nothing required, you would say, but a little
patience and a taste for exercise and bad air.
To breathe dust and bombazine, to feed the
mind on cackling gossip, to hear three parts of
a case and drink a glass of sherry, to long with
indescribable longings for the hour when a man
may slip out of his travesty and devote himself
to golf for the rest of the afternoon, and to
do this day by day and year after year, may
seem so small a thing to the inexperienced!
But those who have made the experiment are
of a different way of thinking, and count it the
most arduous form of idleness.

More swing doors open into pigeon-holes
where Judges of the First Appeal sit singly,
and halls of audience where the supreme Lords

sit by three or four. Here, you may see
Scott's place within the bar, where he wrote
many a page of Waverley novels to the drone
of judicial proceeding. You will hear a good
deal of shrewdness, and, as their Lordships do
not altogether disdain pleasantry, a fair proportion of dry fun. The broadest of broad Scotch
is now banished from the bench ; but the courts
still retain a certain national flavour. We have
a solemn enjoyable way of lingering on a case.
We treat law as a fine art, and relish and
digest a good distinction. There is no hurry:
point after point must be rightly examined
and reduced to principle ; judge after judge
must utter forth his *obiter dicta* to delighted
brethren.

Besides the courts, there are installed under
the same roof no less than three libraries: two
of no mean order ; confused and semi-subter-
ranean, full of stairs and galleries ; where
you may see the most studious-looking wigs
fishing out novels by lanthorn light, in the

Library beneath the Parliament Hall

very place where the old Privy Council tor-
tured Covenanters. As the Parliament House

is built upon a slope, although it presents only one story to the north, it measures half-a-dozen at least upon the south ; and range after range of vaults extend below the libraries. Few places are more characteristic of this hilly capital. You descend one stone stair after another, and wander, by the flicker of a match, in a labyrinth of stone cellars. Now, you pass below the Outer Hall and hear overhead, brisk but ghostly, the interminable pattering of legal feet. Now, you come upon a strong door with a wicket : on the other side are the cells of the police office and the trap-stair that gives admittance to the dock in the Justiciary Court. Many a foot that has gone up there lightly enough, has been dead-heavy in the descent. Many a man's life has been argued away from him during long hours in the court above. But just now that tragic stage is empty and silent like a church on a week-day, with the bench all sheeted up and nothing moving but the sunbeams on the wall. A little farther and you strike upon a room, not empty like the rest, but crowded with *productions* from bygone criminal cases ; a grim lumber : lethal weapons, poisoned organs in a jar, a door with a shot hole through the panel, behind which a man fell dead. I cannot fancy why they should preserve them, unless it were against the Judgment Day. At length, as you continue to descend, you see a peep of yellow gaslight and hear a jostling, whispering noise ahead ; next moment you turn a corner, and there, in a whitewashed passage, is a machinery belt industriously turning on its wheels. You would think the engine had grown there of its own accord, like a cellar fungus, and would soon spin itself out and fill the vaults from end to end with its mysterious labours. In truth, it is only some gear of the steam ventilator ; and you will find the engineers at hand, and may step out of their door into the sunlight. For all this while, you have not been descending

towards the earth's centre, be ly to the
bottom of the hill and the foundations of the
Parliament House ; low down to be sure, but
still under the open heaven and in a field of
grass. The daylight shines garishly on the
back windows of the Irish quarter ; on broken
shutters, wry gables, old palsied houses on the
brink of ruin, a crumbling human pig-sty fit
for human pigs. There are few signs of life,
besides a scanty washing or a face at a window:
the dwellers are abroad, but they will return at
night and stagger to their pallets.

CHAPTER IV

LEGENDS

THE character of a place is often most perfectly expressed in its associations. An event strikes root and grows into a legend, when it has happened amongst congenial surroundings. Ugly actions, above all in ugly places, have the true romantic quality, and become an undying property of their scene. To a man like Scott, the different appearances of nature seemed each to contain its own legend ready made, which it was his to call forth : in such or such a place, only such or such events ought with propriety to happen ; and in this spirit he made the *Lady of the Lake* for Ben Venue, the *Heart of Midlothian* for Edinburgh, and the *Pirate*, so indifferently written but so romantically conceived, for the desolate islands and roaring tideways of the North. The common run of mankind have, from generation to generation, an instinct almost as delicate as that of Scott; but where he created new things, they only forget what is unsuitable among the old ; and by survival of the fittest, a body of tradition becomes a work of art. So, in the low dens and high-flying garrets of Edinburgh, people may go back upon dark passages in the town's adventures, and chill their marrow with winter's tales about the fire : tales that are singularly apposite and characteristic, not only of the old life, but of the very constitution of built nature in that part, and singularly well qualified to add horror to horror, when the wind pipes around the tall lands, and hoots adown arched passages, and the far-spread wilderness of city lamps keeps quavering and flaring in the gusts.

Here, it is the tale of Begbie the bank-porter, stricken to the heart at a blow and left

THE
CANONGATE
TOLBOOTH

in his blood within a step or two of the
crowded High Street. There, people hush
their voices over Burke and Hare ; over drugs
and violated graves, and the resurrection-men
smothering their victims with their knees.
Here, again, the fame of Deacon Brodie is
kept piously fresh. A great man in his day
was the Deacon ; well seen in good society,
crafty with his hands as a cabinetmaker, and
one who could sing a song with taste. Many
a citizen was proud to welcome the Deacon
to supper, and dismissed him with regret at
a timeous hour, who would have been vastly
disconcerted had he known how soon, and in
what guise, his visitor returned. Many stories
are told of this redoubtable Edinburgh burglar,
but the one I have in my mind most vividly
gives the key of all the rest. A friend of
Brodie's, nested some way towards heaven in
one of these great *lands*, had told him of a
projected visit to the country, and afterwards
detained by some affairs, put it off and stayed

the night in town. The good man had lain some time awake; it was far on in the small hours by the Tron bell ; when suddenly there came a creak, a jar, a faint light. Softly he clambered out of bed and up to a false window which looked upon another room, and there, by the glimmer of a thieves' lantern, was his good friend the Deacon in a mask. It is characteristic of the town and the town's manners that this little episode should have been quietly tided over, and quite a good time elapsed before a great robbery, an escape, a Bow Street runner, a cock-fight, an apprehension in a cupboard in Amsterdam, and a last step into the air off his own greatly-improved gallows drop, brought the career of Deacon William Brodie to an end. But still, by the mind's eye, he may be seen, a man harassed below a mountain of duplicity, slinking from a magistrate's supper-room to a thieves' ken, and pickeering among the closes by the flicker of a dark lamp.

Cockburn Street

Or where the Deacon is out of favour, perhaps some memory lingers of the great plagues, and of fatal houses still unsafe to enter within the memory of man. For in time of pestilence the discipline had been sharp and sudden, and what we now call 'stamping out contagion' was carried on with deadly rigour. The officials, in their gowns of grey, with a white St. Andrew's cross on back and breast, and a white cloth carried before them on a staff, perambulated the city, adding the terror of man's justice to the fear of God's visitation. The dead they buried on the Borough Muir; the living who had concealed the sickness were drowned, if they were women, in the Quarry Holes, and if they were men, were hanged and gibbeted at their own doors ; and wherever the evil had passed, furniture was destroyed and houses closed. And the most bogeyish part of the story is about such houses. Two generations back they still stood dark and empty; people avoided them as they passed

THE LAWN MARKET

by; the boldest schoolboy only shouted through the keyhole and made off; for within, it was supposed, the plague lay ambushed like a basilisk, ready to flow forth and spread blain and pustule through the city. What a terrible next-door neighbour for superstitious citizens! A rat scampering within would send a shudder through the stoutest heart. Here, if you like, was a sanitary parable, addressed by our uncleanly forefathers to their own neglect.

And then we have Major Weir; for although even his house is now demolished, old Edinburgh cannot clear herself of his unholy memory. He and his sister lived together in an odour of sour piety. She was a marvellous spinster; he had a rare gift of supplication, and was known among devout admirers by the name of Angelical Thomas. 'He was a tall, black man, and ordinarily looked down to the ground; a grim countenance, and a big nose. His garb still a cloak, and somewhat dark, and he never

went without his staff.' How it came about
that Angelical Thomas was burned in company
with his staff, and his sister in gentler manner
hanged, and whether these two were simply
religious maniacs of the more furious order,
or had real as well as imaginary sins upon
their old-world shoulders, are points happily
beyond the reach of our intention. At least,
it is suitable enough that out of this superstitious city some such example should have
been put forth: the outcome and fine flower
of dark and vehement religion. And at least
the facts struck the public fancy and brought
forth a remarkable family of myths. It would
appear that the Major's staff went upon his
errands, and even ran before him with a
lantern on dark nights. Gigantic females,
'stentoriously laughing and gaping with tehees
of laughter' at unseasonable hours of night
and morning, haunted the purlieus of his
abode. His house fell under such a load of
infamy that no one dared to sleep in it, until

The
Advocate's
Close
—
High
Street

G

municipal improvement levelled the structure with the ground. And my father has often been told in the nursery how the devil's coach, drawn by six coal-black horses with fiery eyes, would drive at night into the West Bow, and belated people might see the dead Major through the glasses.

Another legend is that of the two maiden sisters. A legend I am afraid it may be, in the most discreditable meaning of the term; or perhaps something worse—a mere yester-day's fiction. But it is a story of some vitality, and is worthy of a place in the Edinburgh kalendar. This pair inhabited a single room; from the facts, it must have been double-bedded; and it may have been of some dimensions: but when all is said, it was a single room. Here our two spinsters fell out—on some point of controversial divinity belike: but fell out so bitterly that there was never a word spoken between them, black or white, from that day forward. You would

have thought they would separate : but no ;
whether from lack of means, or the Scottish
fear of scandal, they continued to keep house
together where they were. A chalk line
drawn upon the floor separated their two
domains ; it bisected the doorway and the
fireplace, so that each could go out and in,
and do her cooking without violating the
territory of the other. So, for years, they
coexisted in a hateful silence ; their meals,
their ablutions, their friendly visitors, exposed
to an unfriendly scrutiny ; and at night, in
the dark watches, each could hear the breath-
ing of her enemy. Never did four walls
look down upon an uglier spectacle than
these sisters rivalling in unsisterliness. Here
is a canvas for Hawthorne to have turned
into a cabinet picture—he had a Puritanic
vein, which would have fitted him to treat
this Puritanic horror ; he could have shown
them to us in their sicknesses and at their
hideous twin devotions, thumbing a pair

of great Bibles, or praying aloud for each other's penitence with marrowy emphasis; now each, with kilted petticoat, at her own corner of the fire on some tempestuous evening; now sitting each at her window, looking out upon the summer landscape sloping far below them towards the firth, and the field-paths where they had wandered hand in hand; or, as age and infirmity grew upon them and prolonged their toilettes, and their hands began to tremble and their heads to nod involuntarily, growing only the more steeled in enmity with years; until one fine day, at a word, a look, a visit, or the approach of death, their hearts would melt and the chalk boundary be overstepped for ever.

Alas! to those who know the ecclesiastical history of the race——the most perverse and melancholy in man's annals—this will seem only a figure of much that is typical of Scotland and her high-seated capital above the Forth—a figure so grimly realistic that it may pass with strangers for a caricature. We are wonderful patient haters for conscience' sake up here in the North. I spoke, in the first of these papers, of the Parliaments of the Established and Free Churches, and how they can hear each other singing psalms across the street. There is but a street between them in space, but a shadow between them in principle; and yet there they sit, enchanted, and in damnatory accents pray for each other's growth in grace. It would be well if there were no more than two; but the sects in Scotland form a large family of sisters, and the chalk lines are thickly drawn, and run through the midst of many private homes. Edinburgh is a city of churches, as though it were a place of pilgrimage. You will see four within a stone-cast at the head of the West Bow. Some are crowded to the doors; some are empty like monuments; and yet you will ever find new ones in the building. Hence that sur-

High Street,

from the Netherbow

prising clamour of church bells that suddenly breaks out upon the Sabbath morning, from Trinity and the sea-skirts to Morningside on the borders of the hills. I have heard the chimes of Oxford playing their symphony in a golden autumn morning, and beautiful it was to hear. But in Edinburgh all manner of loud bells join, or rather disjoin, in one swelling, brutal babblement of noise. Now one overtakes another, and now lags behind it; now five or six all strike on the pained tympanum at the same punctual instant of time, and make together a dismal chord of discord; and now for a second all seem to have conspired to hold their peace. Indeed, there are not many uproars in this world more dismal than that of the Sabbath bells in Edinburgh: a harsh ecclesiastical tocsin; the outcry of incongruous orthodoxies, calling on every separate conventicler to put up a protest each in his own synagogue, against 'right-hand extremes and left-hand defections.' And surely there are few worse extremes than this extremity of zeal; and few more deplorable defections than this disloyalty to Christian love. Shakespeare wrote a comedy of 'Much Ado about Nothing.' The Scottish nation made a fantastic tragedy on the same subject. And it is for the success of this remarkable piece that these bells are sounded every Sabbath morning on the hills above the Forth. How many of them might rest silent in the steeple, how many of these ugly churches might be demolished and turned once more into useful building material, if people who think almost exactly the same thoughts about religion would condescend to worship God under the same roof! But there are the chalk lines. And which is to pocket pride, and speak the foremost word?

CHAPTER V

IT was Queen Mary who threw open the
gardens of the Greyfriars: a new and
semi-rural cemetery in those days, although it
has grown an antiquity in its turn and been
superseded by half-a-dozen others. The Friars
must have had a pleasant time on summer
evenings ; for their gardens were situated to
a wish, with the tall castle and the tallest of
the castle crags in front. Even now, it is one
of our famous Edinburgh points of view;
and strangers are led thither to see, by yet
another instance, how strangely the city lies
upon her hills. The enclosure is of an irregular shape ; the double church of Old and

New Greyfriars stands on the level at the top; a few thorns are dotted here and there, and the ground falls by terrace and steep slope towards the north. The open shows many slabs and table tombstones; and all round the margin, the place is girt by an array of aristocratic mausoleums appallingly adorned.

Setting aside the tombs of Roubilliac, which belong to the heroic order of graveyard art, we Scotch stand, to my fancy, highest among nations in the matter of grimly illustrating death. We seem to love for their own sake the emblems of time and the great change; and even around country churches you will find a wonderful exhibition of skulls, and crossbones, and noseless angels, and trumpets pealing for the Judgment Day. Every mason was a pedestrian Holbein: he had a deep consciousness of death, and loved to put its terrors pithily before the churchyard loiterer; he was brimful of rough hints upon mortality, and any dead farmer was seized upon

Tombs in Greyfriars

to be a text. The classical examples of this art are in Greyfriars. In their time, these were doubtless costly monuments, and reckoned of a very elegant proportion by contemporaries; and now, when the elegance is not so apparent, the significance remains. You may perhaps look with a smile on the profusion of Latin mottoes—some crawling endwise up the shaft of a pillar, some issuing on a scroll from angels' trumpets—on the emblematic horrors, the figures rising headless from the grave, and all the traditional ingenuities in which it pleased our fathers to set forth their sorrow for the dead and their sense of earthly mutability. But it is not a hearty sort of mirth. Each ornament may have been executed by the merriest apprentice, whistling as he plied the mallet; but the original meaning of each, and the combined effect of so many of them in this quiet enclosure, is serious to the point of melancholy.

Round a great part of the circuit, houses of a

H

low class present their backs to the churchyard. Only a few inches separate the living from the dead. Here, a window is partly blocked up by the pediment of a tomb; there, where the street falls far below the level of the graves, a chimney has been trained up the back of a monument, and a red pot looks vulgarly over from behind. A damp smell of the graveyard finds its way into houses where workmen sit at meat. Domestic life on a small scale goes forward visibly at the windows. The very solitude and stillness of the enclosure, which lies apart from the town's traffic, serves to accentuate the contrast. As you walk upon the graves, you see children scattering crumbs to feed the sparrows; you hear people singing or washing dishes, or the sound of tears and castigation; the linen on a clothespole flaps against funereal sculpture; or perhaps the cat slips over the lintel and descends on a memorial urn. And as there is nothing else astir, these incongruous sights and noises take hold on the attention and exaggerate the sadness of the place.

Greyfriars is continually overrun by cats. I

Tomb in Greyfriars

have seen one afternoon, as many as thirteen of them seated on the grass beside old Milne, the Master Builder, all sleek and fat, and complacently blinking, as if they had fed upon strange meats. Old Milne was chaunting with the saints, as we may hope, and cared little for the company about his grave; but I confess the spectacle had an ugly side for me; and I was glad to step forward and raise my eyes to where the Castle and the roofs of the Old Town, and the spire of the Assembly Hall, stood deployed against the sky with the colourless precision of engraving. An open outlook is to be desired from a churchyard, and a sight of the sky and some of the world's beauty relieves a mind from morbid thoughts.

I shall never forget one visit. It was a grey, dropping day; the grass was strung with rain-drops; and the people in the houses kept hanging out their shirts and petticoats and angrily taking them in again, as the weather turned from wet to fair and back again. A gravedigger and a friend of his, a gardener from the country, accompanied me into one after another of the cells and little courtyards in which

it gratified the wealthy of old days to enclose
their old bones from neighbourhood. In one,
under a sort of shrine, we found a forlorn
human effigy, very realistically executed down
to the detail of his ribbed stockings, and hold-
ing in his hand a ticket with the date
of his demise. He looked most pitiful and
ridiculous, shut up by himself in his aristocratic precinct, like a bad old boy or an
inferior forgotten deity under a new dispensation; the burdocks grew familiarly about his
feet, the rain dripped all round him; and the
world maintained the most entire indifference
as to who he was or whither he had gone.
In another, a vaulted tomb, handsome ex-
ternally but horrible inside with damp and
cobwebs, there were three mounds of black
earth and an uncovered thigh bone. This
was the place of interment, it appeared, of a
family with whom the gardener had been long
in service. He was among old acquaintances.
' This'll be Miss Marg'et's,' said he, giving the

bone a friendly kick. 'The auld —— !' I have always an uncomfortable feeling in a graveyard, at sight of so many tombs to perpetuate memories best forgotten; but I never had the impression so strongly as that day. People had been at some expense in both these cases: to provoke a melancholy feeling of derision in the one, and an insulting epithet in the other. The proper inscription for the most part of mankind, I began to think, is the cynical jeer, *cras tibi*. That, if anything, will stop the mouth of a carper; since it both admits the worst and carries the war triumphantly into the enemy's camp.

Greyfriars is a place of many associations. There was one window in a house at the lower end, now demolished, which was pointed out to me by the gravedigger as a spot of legendary interest. Burke, the resurrection man, infamous for so many murders at five shillings a-head, used to sit thereat, with pipe and nightcap, to watch burials

going forward on the green. In a tomb
higher up, which must then have been but
newly finished, John Knox, according to the
same informant, had taken refuge in a tur-
moil of the Reformation. Behind the church
is the haunted mausoleum of Sir George
Mackenzie : Bloody Mackenzie, Lord Advocate
in the Covenanting troubles and author of some
pleasing sentiments on toleration. Here, in
the last century, an old Heriot's Hospital
boy once harboured from the pursuit of the
police. The hospital is next door to Greyfriars—a courtly building among lawns, where,
on Founder's Day, you may see a multitude
of children playing Kiss-in-the-Ring and
Round the Mulberry-bush. Thus, when the
fugitive had managed to conceal himself in
the tomb, his old schoolmates had a hundred
opportunities to bring him food; and there
he lay in safety till a ship was found to
smuggle him abroad. But his must have
been indeed a heart of brass, to lie all day

and night alone with the dead persecutor; and other lads were far from emulating him in courage. When a man's soul is certainly in hell, his body will scarce lie quiet in a tomb however costly; some time or other the door must open, and the reprobate come forth in the abhorred garments of the grave. It was thought a high piece of prowess to knock at the Lord Advocate's mausoleum and challenge him to appear. 'Bluidy Mackingie, come oot if ye dar'!' sang the foolhardy urchins. But Sir George had other affairs on hand; and the author of an essay on toleration continues to sleep peacefully among the many whom he so intolerantly helped to slay.

For this *infelix campus*, as it is dubbed in one of its own inscriptions— an inscription over which Dr. Johnson passed a critical eye—is in many ways sacred to the memory of the men whom Mackenzie persecuted. It was here, on the flat tombstones, that the Covenant was

signed by an enthusiastic people. In the long
arm of the churchyard that extends to Lauris-
ton, the prisoners from Bothwell Bridge—fed
on bread and water and guarded, life for life,
by vigilant marksmen—lay five months looking for the scaffold or the plantations. And
while the good work was going forward in
the Grassmarket, idlers in Greyfriars might
have heard the throb of the military drums
that drowned the voices of the martyrs. Nor
is this all : for down in the corner farthest
from Sir George, there stands a monument
dedicated, in uncouth Covenanting verse, to
all who lost their lives in that contention.
There is no moorsman shot in a snow shower
beside Irongray or Co'monell; there is not
one of the two hundred who were drowned
off the Orkneys ; nor so much as a poor, over-
driven, Covenanting slave in the American
plantations ; but can lay claim to a share in
that memorial and, if such things interest just
men among the shades, can boast he has a

monument on earth as well as Julius Cæsar
or the Pharaohs. Where they may all lie,
I know not. Far-scattered bones, indeed! But
if the reader cares to learn how some of them
—or some part of some of them—found their
way at length to such honourable sepulture, let
him listen to the words of one who was their
comrade in life and their apologist when they
were dead. Some of the insane controversial
matter I omit, as well as some digressions, but
leave the rest in Patrick Walker's language
and orthography :—

'The never to be forgotten Mr. *James Renwick* told me,
that he was Witness to their Public Murder at the *Gallowlee*,
between *Leith* and *Edinburgh*, when he saw the Hangman
hash and hagg off all their Five Heads, with *Patrick Fore-
man's* Right Hand : Their Bodies were all buried at the
Gallows Foot ; their Heads, with *Patrick's* Hand, were
brought and put upon five Pikes on the *Pleasaunce-Port*. . . .
Mr. *Renwick* told me also that it was the first public Action
that his Hand was at, to conveen Friends, and lift their
murthered Bodies, and carried them to the West Churchyard of *Edinburgh*,'—not Greyfriars, this time,—'and buried
them there. Then they came about the City . . . . and
took down these Five Heads and that Hand ; and Day being

come, they went quickly up the *Pleasaunce*; and when they came to *Lauristoun* Yards, upon the South-side of the City, they durst not venture, being so light, to go and bury their Heads with their Bodies, which they designed; it being present Death, if any of them had been found. *Alexander Tweedie*, a Friend, being with them, who at that Time was Gardner in these Yards, concluded to bury them in his Yard, being in a Box (wrapped in Linen), where they lay 45 Years except 3 Days, being executed upon the 10th of *October* 1681, and found the 7th Day of *October* 1726. That Piece of Ground lay for some Years unlaboured; and trenching it, the Gardner found them, which affrighted him; the Box was consumed. Mr. *Schaw*, the Owner of these Yards, caused lift them, and lay them upon a Table in his Summer-house : Mr. *Schaw's* mother was so kind, as to cut out a Linen-cloth, and cover them. They lay Twelve Days there, where all had Access to see them. *Alexander Tweedie*, the foresaid Gardner, said, when dying, There was a Treasure hid in his Yard, but neither Gold nor Silver. *Daniel Tweedie*, his Son, came along with me to that Yard, and told me that his Father planted a white Rose-bush above them, and farther down the Yard a red Rose-bush, which were more fruitful than any other bush in the Yard. . . . Many came '—to see the heads—' out of Curiosity; yet I rejoiced to see so many concerned grave Men and Women favouring the Dust of our Martyrs. There were Six of us concluded to bury them upon the Nineteenth Day of *October* 1726, and every One of us to acquaint Friends of the Day and Hour, being *Wednesday*, the Day of the Week on which most of them were executed, and at 4 of the clock at night, being the Hour that most of them went to their resting Graves. We caused make a compleat Coffin for them in Black, with four Yards of fine Linen, the way that our Martyrs Corps were managed. . . . Accordingly we kept the aforesaid Day and Hour, and doubled the Linen, and laid the Half of it below them, their nether Jaws being parted from their Heads ; but being young Men, their Teeth remained. All were Witness to the Holes in each of their Heads, which the Hangman broke with his Hammer ; and according to the Bigness of their Sculls, we laid the Jaws to them, and drew the other Half of the Linen above them, and stufft the Coffin with Shavings. Some prest hard to go thorow the chief Parts of the City as was done at the Revolution ; but this we refused, considering that it looked airy and frothy, to make such Show of them, and inconsistent with the solid serious Observing of such an affecting, surprizing unheard-of Dispensation : But took the ordinary Way of other Burials from that Place, to wit, we went east the Back of the Wall, and in at *Bristo-Port*, and down the Way to the Head of the *Cowgate*, and turned up to the Church-yard, where they were interred close to the Martyrs Tomb, with the greatest Multitude of People Old and Young, Men and Women, Ministers and others, that ever I saw together.'

And so there they were at last, in ' their resting graves.' So long as men do their duty, even if it be greatly in a misapprehension, they will be leading pattern lives ; and

The Communion in a Scottish Church

whether or not they come to lie beside a
martyr's monument, we may be sure they
will find a safe haven somewhere in the pro-
vidence of God. It is not well to think
of death, unless we temper the thought with
that of heroes who despised it. Upon what
ground, is of small account; if it be only
the bishop who was burned for his faith in
the antipodes, his memory lightens the heart
and makes us walk undisturbed among graves.
And so the martyrs' monument is a whole-
some heartsome spot in the field of the dead;
and as we look upon it, a brave influence
comes to us from the land of those who have
won their discharge and, in another phrase
of Patrick Walker's, got 'cleanly off the
stage.'

CHAPTER VI

IT is as much a matter of course to decry the New Town as to exalt the Old ; and the most celebrated authorities have picked out this quarter as the very emblem of what is condemnable in architecture. Much may be said, much indeed has been said, upon the text ; but to the unsophisticated, who call anything pleasing if it only pleases them, the New Town of Edinburgh seems, in itself, not only gay and airy, but highly picturesque. An old skipper, invincibly ignorant of all theories of the sublime and beautiful, once propounded as his most radiant notion for Paradise : 'The New Town of Edinburgh, with the wind the

I

matter of a point free.' He has now gone to that sphere where all good tars are promised pleasant weather in the song, and perhaps his thoughts fly somewhat higher. But there are bright and temperate days—with soft air coming from the inland hills, military music sounding bravely from the hollow of the gardens, the flags all waving on the palaces of Princes Street—when I have seen the town through a sort of glory, and shaken hands in sentiment with the old sailor. And indeed, for a man who has been much tumbled round Orcadian skerries, what scene could be more agreeable to witness ? On such a day, the valley wears a surprising air of festival. It seems (I do not know how else to put my meaning) as if it were a trifle too good to be true. It is what Paris ought to be. It has the scenic quality that would best set off a life of unthinking, open-air diversion. It was meant by nature for the realisation of the society of comic operas. And you can imagine, if the climate were but towardly, how all the world and his wife would flock into these gardens in the cool of the evening, to hear cheerful music, to sip pleasant drinks, to see the moon rise from behind Arthur's Seat and shine upon the spires and monuments and the green tree-tops in the valley. Alas ! and the next morning the rain is splashing on the window, and the passengers flee along Princes Street before the galloping squalls.

It cannot be denied that the original design was faulty and short-sighted, and did not fully profit by the capabilities of the situation. The architect was essentially a town bird, and he laid out the modern city with a view to street scenery, and to street scenery alone. The country did not enter into his plan; he had never lifted his eyes to the hills. If he had so chosen, every street upon the northern slope might have been a noble terrace and commanded an extensive and beautiful view. But the space has been too closely built; many of the houses front the wrong way, intent, like

the Man with the Muck-Rake, on what is not
worth observation, and standing discourteously
back-foremost in the ranks; and in a word, it
is too often only from attic windows, or here

George Street

and there at a crossing, that you can get a
look beyond the city upon its diversified surroundings. But perhaps it is all the more
surprising, to come suddenly on a corner, and see

a perspective of a mile or more of falling street, and beyond that woods and villas, and a blue arm of sea, and the hills upon the farther side.

Hanover Street

Fergusson, our Edinburgh poet, Burns's model, once saw a butterfly at the Town Cross ; and the sight inspired him with a worthless little ode. This painted country man, the dandy of the rose garden, looked far abroad in such a humming neighbourhood ; and you can fancy what moral considerations

a youthful poet would supply. But the in-
cident, in a fanciful sort of way, is characteristic of the place. Into no other city does
the sight of the country enter so far ; if you
do not meet a butterfly, you shall certainly
catch a glimpse of far-away trees upon your
walk ; and the place is full of theatre tricks
in the way of scenery. You peep under an
arch, you descend stairs that look as if they
would land you in a cellar, you turn to the
back-window of a grimy tenement in a lane :—
and behold ! you are face-to-face with distant
and bright prospects. You turn a corner, and
there is the sun going down into the Highland
hills. You look down an alley, and see ships
tacking for the Baltic.

For the country people to see Edinburgh
on her hill-tops, is one thing ; it is another
for the citizen, from the thick of his affairs, to
overlook the country. It should be a genial
and ameliorating influence in life ; it should
prompt good thoughts and remind him

of Nature's unconcern : that he can watch from day to day, as he trots officeward, how the Spring green brightens in the wood or the field grows black under a moving plough-share. I have been tempted, in this con-nexion, to deplore the slender faculties of the human race, with its penny-whistle of a voice, its dull ears, and its narrow range of sight. If you could see as people are to see in heaven, if you had eyes such as you can fancy for a superior race, if you could take clear note of the objects of vision, not only a few yards, but a few miles from where you stand :—think how agreeably your sight would be entertained, how pleasantly your thoughts would be diversified, as you walked the Edinburgh streets ! For you might pause, in some business perplexity, in the midst of the city traffic, and perhaps catch the eye of a shepherd as he sat down to breathe upon a heathery shoulder of the Pentlands ; or per-haps some urchin, clambering in a country elm.

would put aside the leaves and show you his

A Newhaven Fisher

flushed and rustic visage; or a fisher racing
seawards, with the tiller under his elbow,

and the sail sounding in the wind, would fling you a salutation from between Anst'er and the May.

To be old is not the same thing as to be picturesque; nor because the Old Town bears a strange physiognomy, does it at all follow that the New Town shall look commonplace. Indeed, apart from antique houses, it is curious how much description would apply commonly to either. The same sudden accidents of ground, a similar dominating site above the plain, and the same superposition of one rank of society over another, are to be observed in both. Thus, the broad and comely approach to Princes Street from the east, lined with hotels and public offices, makes a leap over the gorge of the Low Calton; if you cast a glance over the parapet, you look direct into that sunless and disreputable confluent of Leith Street; and the same tall houses open upon both thoroughfares. This is only the New Town passing overhead above its own cellars;

walking, so to speak, over its own children, as is the way of cities and the human race.

Leith Street, from Regent's Bridge.

But at the Dean Bridge, you may behold a spectacle of a more novel order. The river runs at the bottom of a deep valley, among

rocks and between gardens; the crest of either
bank is occupied by some of the most com-

Regent's Bridge

modious streets and crescents in the modern
city; and a handsome bridge unites the two

summits. Over this, every afternoon, private
carriages go spinning by, and ladies with card-
cases pass to and fro about the duties of society.
And yet down below, you may still see, with
its mills and foaming weir, the little rural

VIEW
from the
DEAN BRIDGE

village of Dean. Modern improvement has
gone overhead on its high-level viaduct; and
the extended city has cleanly overleapt, and
left unaltered, what was once the summer
retreat of its comfortable citizens. Every town
embraces hamlets in its growth; Edinburgh

herself has embraced a good few; but it is strange to see one still surviving—and to see it some hundreds of feet below your path. Is it Torre del Greco that is built above buried Herculaneum? Herculaneum was dead at least; but the sun still shines upon the roofs of Dean; the smoke still rises thriftily from its chimneys; the dusty miller comes to his door, looks at the gurgling water, hearkens to the turning wheel and the birds about the shed, and perhaps whistles an air of his own to enrich the symphony—for all the world as if Edinburgh were still the old Edinburgh on the Castle Hill, and Dean were still the quietest of hamlets buried a mile or so in the green country.

It is not so long ago since magisterial David Hume lent the authority of his example to the exodus from the Old Town, and took up his new abode in a street which is still (so oddly may a jest become perpetuated) known as Saint David Street. Nor is the town so

large but a holiday schoolboy may harry a
bird's nest within half a mile of his own door.
There are places that still smell of the plough
in memory's nostrils. Here, one had heard a
blackbird on a hawthorn ; there, another was
taken on summer evenings to eat strawberries
and cream ; and you have seen a waving
wheatfield on the site of your present residence.
The memories of an Edinburgh boy are but
partly memories of the town. I look back
with delight on many an escalade of garden
walls ; many a ramble among lilacs full of
piping birds ; many an exploration in obscure
quarters that were neither town nor country ;
and I think that both for my companions and
myself, there was a special interest, a point of
romance, and a sentiment as of foreign travel,
when we hit in our excursions on the butt-end
of some former hamlet, and found a few rustic
cottages embedded among streets and squares.
The tunnel to the Scotland Street Station, the
sight of the trains shooting out of its dark

maw with the two guards upon the brake, the thought of its length and the many ponderous edifices and open thoroughfares above, were certainly things of paramount impressiveness to a young mind. It was a subterranean passage, although of a larger bore than we were accustomed to in Ainsworth's novels; and these two words, 'subterranean passage,' were in themselves an irresistible attraction, and seemed to bring us nearer in spirit to the heroes we loved and the black rascals we secretly aspired to imitate. To scale the Castle Rock from West Princes Street Gardens, and lay a triumphal hand against the rampart itself, was to taste a high order of romantic pleasure. And there are other sights and exploits which crowd back upon my mind under a very strong illumination of remembered pleasure. But the effect of not one of them all will compare with the discoverer's joy, and the sense of old Time and his slow changes on the face of this earth, with which I explored

such corners as Cannonmills or Water Lane,
or the nugget of cottages at Broughton

The Castle Rock

Market. They were more rural than the
open country, and gave a greater impression

K

of antiquity than the oldest *land* upon the High Street. They too, like Fergusson's butterfly, had a quaint air of having wandered far from their own place; they looked abashed and homely, with their gables and their creeping plants, their outside stairs and running mill-streams; there were corners that smelt like the end of the country garden where I spent my Aprils; and the people stood to gossip at their doors, as they might have done in Colinton or Cramond.

In a great measure we may, and shall, eradicate this haunting flavour of the country. The last elm is dead in Elm Row; and the villas and the workmen's quarters spread apace on all the borders of the city. We can cut down the trees; we can bury the grass under dead paving-stones; we can drive brisk streets through all our sleepy quarters; and we may forget the stories and the playgrounds of our boyhood. But we have some possessions that not even the infuriate zeal of builders can utterly abolish and destroy. Nothing can abolish the hills, unless it be a cataclysm of nature which shall subvert Edinburgh Castle itself and lay all her florid structures in the dust. And as long as we have the hills and the Firth, we have a famous heritage to leave our children. Our windows, at no expense to us, are mostly artfully stained to represent a landscape. And when the Spring comes round, and the hawthorn begins to flower, and the meadows to smell of young grass, even in the thickest of our streets, the country hill-tops find out a young man's eyes, and set his heart beating for travel and pure air.

CHAPTER VII

MR. RUSKIN'S denunciation of the New Town of Edinburgh includes, as I have heard it repeated, nearly all the stone and lime we have to show. Many however find a grand air and something settled and imposing in the better parts ; and upon many, as I have said, the confusion of styles induces an agreeable stimulation of the mind. But upon the subject of our recent villa architecture, I am frankly ready to mingle my tears with Mr. Ruskin's, and it is a subject which makes one envious of his large declamatory and controversial eloquence.

Day by day, one new villa, one new object

of offence, is added to another; all around Newington and Morningside, the dismallest structures keep springing up like mushrooms; the pleasant hills are loaded with them, each impudently squatted in its garden, each roofed and carrying chimneys like a house. And yet a glance of an eye discovers their true character. They are not houses; for they were not designed with a view to human habitation, and the internal arrangements are, as they tell me, fantastically unsuited to the needs of man. They are not buildings; for you can scarcely say a thing is built where every measurement is in clamant disproportion with its neighbour. They belong to no style of art, only to a form of business much to be regretted.

Why should it be cheaper to erect a structure where the size of the windows bears no rational relation to the size of the front? Is there any profit in a misplaced chimney-stalk? Does a hard-working, greedy builder gain more on a monstrosity than on a decent cottage of equal

plainness ? Frankly, we should say, No. Bricks
may be omitted, and green timber employed,
in the construction of even a very elegant
design ; and there is no reason why a chimney
should be made to vent, because it is so
situated as to look comely from without. On
the other hand, there is a noble way of being
ugly : a high-aspiring fiasco like the fall of
Lucifer. There are daring and gaudy buildings that manage to be offensive, without
being contemptible ; and we know that ' fools
rush in where angels fear to tread.' But to
aim at making a common-place villa, and to
make it insufferably ugly in each particular ;
to attempt the homeliest achievement and to
attain the bottom of derided failure ; not to
have any theory but profit and yet, at an
equal expense, to outstrip all competitors in
the art of conceiving and rendering permanent
deformity ; and to do all this in what is, by
nature, one of the most agreeable neighbour-
hoods in Britain :—what are we to say, but

that this also is a distinction, hard to earn although not greatly worshipful?

Indifferent buildings give pain to the sensitive; but these things offend the plainest taste. It is a danger which threatens the amenity of the town; and as this eruption keeps spreading on our borders, we have ever the farther to walk among unpleasant sights, before we gain the country air. If the population of Edinburgh were a living, autonomous body, it would arise like one man and make night hideous with arson; the builders and their accomplices would be driven to work, like the Jews of yore, with the trowel in one hand and the defensive cutlass in the other; and as soon as one of these masonic wonders had been consummated, right-minded iconoclasts should fall thereon and make an end of it at once.

Possibly these words may meet the eye of a builder or two. It is no use asking them to employ an architect; for that would be to touch them in a delicate quarter, and its use would largely depend on what architect they were minded to call in. But let them get any architect in the world to point out any reasonably well-proportioned villa, not his own design; and let them reproduce that model to satiety.

CHAPTER VIII

THE CALTON HILL

THE east of new Edinburgh is guarded by a craggy hill, of no great elevation, which the town embraces. The old London road runs on one side of it; while the New Approach, leaving it on the other hand, completes the circuit. You mount by stairs in a cutting of the rock to find yourself in a field of monuments. Dugald Stewart has the honours of situation and architecture; Burns is memorialised lower down upon a spur; Lord Nelson, as befits a sailor, gives his name to the topgallant of the Calton Hill. This latter erection has been differently and yet, in both cases, aptly compared to a telescope and a butterchurn ; comparisons apart, it ranks among the vilest of men's handiworks. But the chief feature is an unfinished range of columns, 'the Modern Ruin' as it has been called, an imposing object from far and near,

The Calton Hill

and giving Edinburgh, even from the sea, that false air of a Modern Athens which has earned for her so many slighting speeches. It was meant to be a National Monument ; and its present state is a very suitable monument to certain national characteristics. The old Observatory—a quaint brown building on the edge of the steep—and the new Observatory —a classical edifice with a dome—occupy the central portion of the summit. All these are scattered on a green turf, browsed over by some sheep.

The scene suggests reflections on fame and on man's injustice to the dead. You see Dugald Stewart rather more handsomely commemorated than Burns. Immediately below, in the Canongate churchyard, lies Robert Fergusson, Burns's master in his art, who died insane while yet a stripling; and if Dugald Stewart has been somewhat too boisterously acclaimed, the Edinburgh poet, on the other hand, is most unrighteously forgotten. The votaries of Burns, a crew too common in all ranks in Scotland and more remarkable for number than discretion, eagerly suppress all mention of the lad who handed to him the poetic impulse and, up to the time when he grew famous, continued to influence him in his manner and the choice of subjects. Burns himself not only acknowledged his debt in a fragment of autobiography, but erected a tomb over the grave in Canongate churchyard. This was worthy of an artist, but it was done in vain; and although I think I have read nearly all the biographies of Burns, I cannot remember one in which the modesty of nature was not violated, or where Fergusson was not sacrificed to the credit of his follower's originality. There is a kind of gaping admiration that would fain roll Shakespeare and Bacon into one, to have a bigger thing to gape at; and a class of men who cannot edit one author without disparaging all others. They are indeed mistaken if they think to please the great originals; and whoever puts Fergusson right with fame, cannot do better than dedicate his labours to the memory of Burns, who will be the best delighted of the dead.

Of all places for a view, this Calton Hill is perhaps the best; since you can see the Castle,

Here lies

ROBERT FERGUSSON POET

Born September 5 1751

Died October 16th 1774

No sculptur'd Marble here nor pompous lay
No storied Urn nor animated Bust
This simple Stone directs Ble Scotia's way
To pour her Sorrows o'er her Poet's Dust.

Tombstone
erected by BURNS
over FERGUSSON'S
          GRAVE
in the CANONGATE
          CHURCHYARD

which you lose from the Castle, and Arthur's Seat, which you cannot see from Arthur's Seat. It is the place to stroll on one of those days of sunshine and east wind which are so common in our more than temperate summer. The breeze comes off the sea, with a little of the freshness, and that touch of chill, peculiar to the quarter, which is delightful to certain very ruddy organizations and greatly the reverse to the majority of mankind. It brings with it a faint, floating haze, a cunning decolourizer, although not thick enough to obscure outlines near at hand. But the haze lies more thickly to windward at the far end of Musselburgh Bay; and over the Links of Aberlady and Berwick Law and the hump of the Bass Rock it assumes the aspect of a bank of thin sea fog.

Immediately underneath upon the south, you command the yards of the High School, and the towers and courts of the new Jail—a large place, castellated to the extent of folly, standing by itself on the edge of a steep cliff, and often joyfully hailed by tourists as the Castle. In the one, you may perhaps see female prisoners taking exercise like a string of nuns; in the other, schoolboys running at play and their shadows keeping step with them. From the bottom of the valley, a gigantic chimney rises almost to the level of the eye, a taller and a shapelier edifice than Nelson's Monument. Look a little farther, and there is Holyrood Palace, with its Gothic frontal and ruined abbey, and the red sentry pacing smartly to and fro before the door like a mechanical figure in a panorama. By way of an outpost, you can single out the little peak-roofed lodge, over which Rizzio's murderers made their escape and where Queen Mary herself, according to gossip, bathed in white wine to entertain her loveliness. Behind and overhead, lie the Queen's Park, from Muschat's Cairn to Dumbiedykes, St. Margaret's Loch, and the long wall of Salisbury Crags; and thence, by knoll and rocky

The
Chapel
Royal

T. H. CRAWFORD
J. T. BAILLIE

L

bulwark and precipitous slope, the eye rises to the top of Arthur's Seat, a hill for magnitude, a mountain in virtue of its bold design. This upon your left. Upon the right, the roofs and spires of the Old Town climb one above another to where the citadel prints its broad bulk and jagged crown of bastions on the western sky.— Perhaps it is now one in the afternoon; and at the same instant of time, a ball rises to the summit of Nelson's flagstaff close at hand, and, far away, a puff of smoke followed by a report bursts from the half-moon battery at the Castle. This is the time-gun by which people set their watches, as far as the sea coast or in hill farms upon the Pentlands.—To complete the view, the eye enfilades Princes Street, black with traffic, and has a broad look over the valley between the Old Town and the New: here, full of railway trains and stepped over by the high North Bridge upon its many columns, and there, green with trees and gardens.

On the north, the Calton Hill is neither so

abrupt in itself nor has it so exceptional an out-look; and yet even here it commands a striking prospect. A gully separates it from the New Town. This is Greenside, where witches were burned and tournaments held in former days. Down that almost precipitous bank, Bothwell launched his horse, and so first, as they say, attracted the bright eyes of Mary. It is now tesselated with sheets and blankets out to dry, and the sound of people beating carpets is rarely absent. Beyond all this, the suburbs run out to Leith; Leith camps on the sea-side with her forest of masts; Leith roads are full of ships at anchor; the sun picks out the white pharos upon Inchkeith Island; the Firth extends on either hand from the Ferry to the May; the towns of Fifeshire sit, each in its bank of blowing smoke, along the opposite coast; and the hills inclose the view, except to the farthest east, where the haze of the horizon rests upon the open sea. There lies the road to Norway: a dear road for Sir

PRINCES STREET.

Patrick Spens and his Scots Lords ; and yonder smoke on the hither side of Largo Law is Aberdour, from whence they sailed to seek a queen for Scotland.

> ' O, lang, lang, may the ladies sit,
>> Wi' their fans into their hand,
> Or ere they see Sir Patrick Spens
>> Come sailing to the land ! '

The sight of the sea, even from a city, will bring thoughts of storm and sea disaster. The sailors' wives of Leith and the fisherwomen of Cockenzie, not sitting languorously with fans, but crowding to the tail of the harbour with a shawl about their ears, may still look vainly for brave Scotsmen who will return no more, or boats that have gone on their last fishing. Since Sir Patrick sailed from Aberdour, what a multitude have gone down in the North Sea ! Yonder is Auldhame, where the London smack went ashore and wreckers cut the rings from ladies' fingers ; and a few miles round Fife Ness is the fatal Inchcape, now a star of guidance ; and the lee shore to the east of the Inchcape, is that

Forfarshire coast where Mucklebackit sorrowed for his son.

These are the main features of the scene roughly sketched. How they are all tilted by the inclination of the ground, how each stands out in delicate relief against the rest, what manifold detail, and play of sun and shadow, animate and accentuate the picture, is a matter for a person on the spot, and turning swiftly on his heels, to grasp and bind together in one comprehensive look. It is the character of such a prospect, to be full of change and of things moving. The multiplicity embarrasses the eye; and the mind, among so much, suffers itself to grow absorbed with single points. You remark a tree in a hedgerow, or follow a cart along a country road. You turn to the city, and see children, dwarfed by distance into pigmies, at play about suburban doorsteps; you have a glimpse upon a thoroughfare where people are densely moving; you note ridge after ridge of chimney-stacks running downhill one behind

another, and church spires rising bravely from
the sea of roofs. At one of the innumerable
windows, you watch a figure moving; on one of
the multitude of roofs, you watch clambering
chimney-sweeps. The wind takes a run and
scatters the smoke; bells are heard, far and near,
faint and loud, to tell the hour; or perhaps a
bird goes dipping evenly over the housetops, like
a gull across the waves. And here you are in
the meantime, on this pastoral hillside, among
nibbling sheep and looked upon by monumental
buildings.

Return thither on some clear, dark, moonless
night, with a ring of frost in the air, and only a
star or two set sparsedly in the vault of heaven;
and you will find a sight as stimulating as the
hoariest summit of the Alps. The solitude
seems perfect; the patient astronomer, flat on
his back under the Observatory dome and spying
heaven's secrets, is your only neighbour; and
yet from all round you there come up the dull
hum of the city, the tramp of countless people

marching out of time, the rattle of carriages and the continuous keen jingle of the tramway bells. An hour or so before, the gas was turned on ; lamplighters scoured the city ; in every house, from kitchen to attic, the windows kindled and gleamed forth into the dusk. And so now, although the town lies blue and darkling on her hills, innumerable spots of the bright element shine far and near along the pavements and upon the high façades. Moving lights of the railway pass and re-pass below the stationary lights upon the bridge. Lights burn in the Jail. Lights burn high up in the tall *lands* and on the Castle turrets, they burn low down in Greenside or along the Park. They run out one beyond the other into the dark country. They walk in a procession down to Leith, and shine singly far along Leith Pier. Thus, the plan of the city and her suburbs is mapped out upon the ground of blackness, as when a child pricks a drawing full of pinholes and exposes it before a candle ; not the darkest night of winter can conceal her

Greenside from the Calton Hill

C. 178.

high station and fanciful design; every evening
in the year she proceeds to illuminate herself
in honour of her own beauty; and as if to
complete the scheme—or rather as if some
prodigal Pharaoh were beginning to extend it
to the adjacent sea and country—half way
over to Fife, there is an outpost of light upon
Inchkeith, and far to seaward, yet another on
the May.

And while you are looking, across upon the
Castle Hill, the drums and bugles begin to recall
the scattered garrison; the air thrills with the
sound; the bugles sing aloud; and the last rising
flourish mounts and melts into the darkness like
a star: a martial swan-song, fitly rounding in the
labours of the day.

CHAPTER IX

WINTER AND NEW YEAR

THE Scotch dialect is singularly rich in terms of reproach against the winter wind. *Snell*, *blae*, *nirly*, and *scowthering*, are four of these significant vocables; they are all words that carry a shiver with them; and for my part as I see them aligned before me on the page, I am persuaded that a big wind comes tearing over the Firth from Burntisland and the northern hills; I think I can hear it howl in the chimney, and as I set my face northwards, feel its smarting kisses on my cheek. Even in the names of places there is often a desolate, inhospitable sound; and I remember two from the near neighbourhood of Edinburgh, Cauldhame and Blaw-weary, that would promise but starving comfort to their inhabitants. The inclemency of heaven, which has thus endowed the language of Scotland with words, has also largely modified the spirit of its poetry. Both poverty and a northern climate teach men the love of the hearth and the sentiment of the family; and the latter, in its own right, inclines a poet to the praise of strong waters. In Scotland, all our singers have a stave or two for blazing fires and stout potations:—to get indoors out of the wind and to swallow something hot to the stomach, are benefits so easily appreciated where they dwelt!

And this is not only so in country districts where the shepherd must wade in the snow all day after his flock, but in Edinburgh itself, and nowhere more apparently stated than in the works of our Edinburgh poet, Fergusson. He was a delicate youth, I take it, and willingly slunk from the robustious

winter to an inn fireside. Love was absent
from his life, or only present, if you prefer,
in such a form that even the least serious of
Burns's amourettes was ennobling by com-
parison ; and so there is nothing to temper the
sentiment of indoor revelry which pervades
the poor boy's verses. Although it is characteristic of his native town, and the manners
of its youth to the present day, this spirit has
perhaps done something to restrict his popularity. He recalls a supper-party pleasantry
with something akin to tenderness ; and
sounds the praises of the act of drinking as if
it were virtuous, or at least witty, in itself.
The kindly jar, the warm atmosphere of
tavern parlours, and the revelry of lawyers'
clerks, do not offer by themselves the materials
of a rich existence. It was not choice, so
much as an external fate, that kept Fergusson
in this round of sordid pleasures. A Scot of
poetic temperament, and without religious
exaltation, drops as if by nature into the

A Night with Fergusson

public-house. The picture may not be pleasing; but what else is a man to do in this dog's weather?

To none but those who have themselves suffered the thing in the body, can the gloom and depression of our Edinburgh winter be brought home. For some constitutions there is something almost physically disgusting in the bleak ugliness of easterly weather; the wind wearies, the sickly sky depresses them; and they turn back from their walk to avoid the aspect of the unrefulgent sun going down among perturbed and pallid mists. The days are so short that a man does much of his business, and certainly all his pleasure, by the haggard glare of gas lamps. The roads are as heavy as a fallow. People go by, so drenched and draggle-tailed that I have often wondered how they found the heart to undress. And meantime the wind whistles through the town as if it were an open meadow; and if you lie awake all night, you hear it shrieking

and raining overhead with a noise of ship-
wrecks and of falling houses.   In a word,
life is so unsightly that there are times when

The
   Castle .

   Rain

the heart turns sick in a man's inside; and
the look of a tavern, or the thought of the
warm, fire-lit study, is like the touch of land to
one who has been long struggling with the seas.

As the weather hardens towards frost, the world begins to improve for Edinburgh people. We enjoy superb sub-arctic sunsets, with the profile of the city stamped in indigo upon a sky of luminous green. The wind may still be cold, but there is a briskness in the air that stirs good blood. People do not all look equally sour and downcast. They fall into two divisions: one, the knight of the blue face and hollow paunch, whom Winter has gotten by the vitals; the other well-lined with New-year's fare, conscious of the touch of cold on his periphery, but stepping through it by the glow of his internal fires. Such an one I remember, triply cased in grease, whom no extremity of temperature could vanquish. 'Well,' would be his jovial salutation, 'here's a sneezer!' And the look of these warm fellows is tonic, and upholds their drooping fellow-townsmen. There is yet another class who do not depend on corporal advantages, but support the winter in virtue of a brave and merry heart. One shivering evening, cold enough for frost but with too high a wind, and a little past sundown, when the lamps were beginning to enlarge their circles in the growing dusk, a brace of barefoot lassies were seen coming eastward in the teeth of the wind. If the one was as much as nine, the other was certainly not more than seven. They were miserably clad; and the pavement was so cold, you would have thought no one could lay a naked foot on it unflinching. Yet they came along waltzing, if you please, while the elder sang a tune to give them music. The person who saw this, and whose heart was full of bitterness at the moment, pocketed a reproof which has been of use to him ever since, and which he now hands on, with his good wishes, to the reader.

At length, Edinburgh, with her satellite hills, and all the sloping country, are sheeted up in white. If it has happened in the dark hours, nurses pluck their children out of bed and run with them to some commanding window,

The Morning Bugle

whence they may see the change that has been worked upon earth's face. ' A ' the hills are covered wi' snaw,' they sing, ' and Winter's noo come fairly ! ' And the children, marvelling at the silence and the white landscape, find a spell appropriate to the season in the words. The reverberation of the snow increases the pale daylight, and brings all objects nearer the eye. The Pentlands are smooth and glittering, with here and there the black ribbon of a dry-stone dyke, and here and there, if there be wind, a cloud of blowing snow upon a shoulder. The Firth seems a leaden creek, that a man might almost jump across, between well-powdered Lothian and well-powdered Fife. And the effect is not, as in other cities, a thing of half a day ; the streets are soon trodden black, but the country keeps its virgin white ; and you have only to lift your eyes and look over miles of country snow. An indescribable cheerfulness breathes about the city; and the well-fed heart sits lightly and beats gaily in the bosom. It is New-year's weather.

New-year's Day, the great national festival,

is a time of family expansions and of deep
carousal. Sometimes, by a sore stroke of fate
for this Calvinistic people, the year's anniver-
sary falls upon a Sunday, when the public-
houses are inexorably closed, when singing and
even whistling is banished from our homes and
highways, and the oldest toper feels called upon
to go to church. Thus pulled about, as if
between two loyalties, the Scotch have to
decide many nice cases of conscience, and ride
the marches narrowly between the weekly and
the annual observance. A party of convivial
musicians, next door to a friend of mine, hung
suspended in this manner on the brink of
their diversions. From ten o'clock on Sunday
night, my friend heard them tuning their
instruments; and as the hour of liberty drew
near, each must have had his music open, his
bow in readiness across the fiddle, his foot
already raised to mark the time, and his
nerves braced for execution; for hardly had
the twelfth stroke sounded from the earliest

steeple, before they had launched forth into a secular bravura.

Currant loaf is now popular eating in all households. For weeks before the great morning, confectioners display stacks of Scotch bun ——a dense, black substance, inimical to life—— and full moons of shortbread adorned with mottoes of peel or sugar-plum in honour of the season and the family affections. ' Frae Auld Reekie,' ' A guid New Year to ye a',' ' For the Auld Folk at Hame,' are among the most favoured of these devices. Can you not see the carrier, after half-a-day's journey on pinching hill-roads, draw up before a cottage in Teviotdale, or perhaps in Manor Glen among the rowans, and the old people receiving the parcel with moist eyes and a prayer for Jock or Jean in the city ? For at this season on the threshold of another year of calamity and stubborn conflict, men feel a need to draw closer the links that unite them ; they reckon the number of their friends, like allies before a war ; and the prayers grow longer in the morning as the absent are recommended by name into God's keeping.

On the day itself, the shops are all shut as on a Sunday ; only taverns, toy-shops, and other holiday magazines, keep open doors. Every one looks for his handsel. The postmen and the lamplighters have left, at every house in their districts, a copy of vernacular verses, asking and thanking in a breath; and it is characteristic of Scotland that these verses may have sometimes a touch of reality in detail or sentiment and a measure of strength in the handling. All over the town, you may see comforter'd schoolboys hastening to squander their half-crowns. There are an infinity of visits to be paid ; all the world is in the street, except the daintier classes ; the sacramental greeting is heard upon all sides ; Auld Lang Syne is much in people's mouths ; and whisky and shortbread are staple articles of consumption. From an early hour a stranger will be impressed by the number of drunken men ; and by afternoon drunkenness has spread to the women. With some classes of society it is as much a matter of duty to drink hard on New-year's Day as to go to church on Sunday. Some have been saving their wages for perhaps a month to do the season honour. Many carry a whisky-bottle in their pocket, which they will press with embarrassing effusion on a perfect stranger. It is inexpedient to risk one's body in a cab, or not, at least, until after a prolonged study of the driver. The streets, which are thronged from end to end, become a place for delicate pilotage. Singly or arm-in-arm, some speech-less, others noisy and quarrelsome, the votaries of the New Year go meandering in and out and cannoning one against another ; and now and again, one falls and lies as he has fallen. Before night, so many have gone to bed or the police office, that the streets seem almost clearer. And as *guisards* and *first-footers* are now not much seen except in country places, when once the New Year has been rung in and proclaimed at the Tron railings, the festivities begin to find their way indoors and something like quiet returns upon the town. But think, in these piled *lands*, of all the senseless snorers, all the broken heads and empty pockets!

Of old, Edinburgh University was the scene of heroic snowballing; and one riot obtained the epic honours of military intervention. But the great generation, I am afraid, is at an end; and even during my own college days, the spirit appreciably declined. Skating and sliding, on the other hand, are honoured more and more; and curling, being a creature of the national genius, is little likely to be disregarded. The patriotism that leads a man to eat Scotch bun will scarce desert him at the curling-pond. Edinburgh, with its long, steep pavements, is the proper home of sliders; many a happy urchin can slide the whole way to school; and the profession of errand boy is transformed into a holiday amusement. As for skating, there is scarce any city so handsomely provided. Duddingstone Loch lies under the abrupt southern

*Duddingstone
in Winter*

side of Arthur's Seat; in summer, a shield of blue, with swans sailing from the reeds; in winter, a field of ringing ice. The village church sits above it on a green promontory; and the village smoke rises from among goodly trees. At the church gates, is the historical

joug, a place of penance for the neck of de-
tected sinners, and the historical *louping-on
stane*, from which Dutch-built lairds and
farmers climbed into the saddle. Here Prince
Charlie slept before the battle of Prestonpans;
and here Deacon Brodie, or one of his gang,
stole a plough coulter before the burglary in
Chessel's Court. On the opposite side of the
loch, the ground rises to Craigmillar Castle,
a place friendly to Stuart Mariolaters. It is
worth a climb, even in summer, to look down
upon the loch from Arthur's Seat; but it is
tenfold more so on a day of skating. The
surface is thick with people moving easily and
swiftly and leaning over at a thousand graceful
inclinations; the crowd opens and closes, and
keeps moving through itself like water; and
the ice rings to half a mile away, with the
flying steel. As night draws on, the single
figures melt into the dusk, until only an obscure stir and coming and going of black
clusters, is visible upon the loch. A little

Craigmillar
Castle

longer, and the first torch is kindled and
begins to flit rapidly across the ice in a ring
of yellow reflection, and this is followed by
another and another, until the whole field is
full of skimming lights.

CHAPTER X

ON three sides of Edinburgh, the country slopes downward from the city, here to the sea, there to the fat farms of Haddington, there to the mineral fields of Linlithgow. On the south alone, it keeps rising until it not only out-tops the Castle but looks down on Arthur's Seat. The character of the neighbourhood is pretty strongly marked by a scarcity of hedges ; by many stone walls of varying height ; by a fair amount of timber, some of it well grown, but apt to be of a bushy, northern profile and poor in foliage; by here and there a little river, Esk or Leith or Almond, busily journeying in the bottom of its glen; and from almost every point, by a peep of the sea or the hills. There is no lack of variety, and yet most of the elements are common to all parts; and the southern district is alone distinguished by considerable summits and a wide view.

From Boroughmuirhead, where the Scottish army encamped before Flodden, the road descends a long hill, at the bottom of which and just as it is preparing to mount upon the other side, it passes a toll-bar and issues at once into the open country. Even as I write these words, they are being antiquated in the progress of events, and the chisels are tinkling on a new row of houses. The builders have at length adventured beyond the toll which held them in respect so long, and proceed to career in these fresh pastures like a herd of colts turned loose. As Lord Beaconsfield proposed to hang an architect by way of stimulation, a man, looking on these doomed meads, imagines a similar example to deter the builders; for it seems as if it must come to an open fight at last to preserve a corner of green country un-bedevilled. And here, appropriately enough, there stood in old days a crow-haunted gibbet, with two bodies hanged in chains. I used to be shown, when a child, a flat stone in the roadway to which the gibbet had been fixed. People of a willing fancy were persuaded, and sought to persuade others, that this stone was never dry. And no wonder, they would add, for the two men had only stolen fourpence between them.

For about two miles the road climbs up-wards, a long hot walk in summer time. You reach the summit at a place where four ways meet, beside the toll of Fairmilehead. The spot is breezy and agreeable both in name and aspect. The hills are close by across a valley : Kirk Yetton, with its long, upright scars visible as far as Fife, and Allermuir the tallest on this side : with wood and tilled field running high upon their borders, and haunches all moulded

into innumerable glens and shelvings and varie-
gated with heather and fern. The air comes
briskly and sweetly off the hills, pure from the
elevation and rustically scented by the upland
plants ; and even at the toll, you may hear the
curlew calling on its mate. At certain seasons,
when the gulls desert their surfy forelands, the
birds of sea and mountain hunt and scream
together in the same field by Fairmilehead.
The winged, wild things intermix their wheel-
ings, the seabirds skim the tree-tops and fish
among the furrows of the plough. These little
craft of air are at home in all the world, so
long as they cruise in their own element ; and
like sailors, ask but food and water from the
shores they coast.

Below, over a stream, the road passes Bow
Bridge, now a dairy-farm, but once a distillery
of whisky. It chanced, some time in the
past century, that the distiller was on terms of
good-fellowship with the visiting officer of
excise. The latter was of an easy, friendly

disposition and a master of convivial arts. Now and again, he had to walk out of Edinburgh to measure the distiller's stock ; and although it was agreeable to find his business lead him in a friend's direction, it was unfortunate that the friend should be a loser by his visits. Accordingly, when he got about the level of Fairmilehead, the gauger would take his flute, without which he never travelled, from his pocket, fit it together, and set manfully to playing, as if for his own delectation and inspired by the beauty of the scene. His favourite air, it seems, was 'Over the hills and far away.' At the first note, the distiller pricked his ears. A flute at Fairmilehead ? and playing 'Over the hills and far away ? ' This must be his friendly enemy, the gauger. Instantly, horses were harnessed, and sundry barrels of whisky were got upon a cart, driven at a gallop round Hill End, and buried in the mossy glen behind Kirk Yetton. In the same breath, you may be sure, a fat fowl was put to the fire, and the whitest napery prepared for the back parlour. A little after, the gauger, having had his fill of music for the moment, came strolling down with the most innocent air imaginable, and found the good people at Bow Bridge taken entirely unawares by his arrival, but none the less glad to see him. The distiller's liquor and the gauger's flute would combine to speed the moments of digestion ; and when both were somewhat mellow, they would wind up the evening with ' Over the hills and far away ' to an accompaniment of knowing glances. And at least, there is a smuggling story, with original and half-idyllic features.

A little further, the road to the right passes an upright stone in a field. The country people call it General Kay's monument. According to them, an officer of that name had perished there in battle at some indistinct period before the beginning of history. The date is reassuring ; for I think cautious writers are silent on the General's exploits. But the stone is connected with one of those remarkable tenures of land which linger on into the modern world from Feudalism. Whenever the reigning sovereign passes by, a certain landed proprietor is held bound to climb on to the top, trumpet in hand, and sound a flourish according to the measure of his knowledge in that art. Happily for a respectable family, crowned heads have no great business in the Pentland Hills. But the story lends a character of comicality to the stone ; and the passer-by will sometimes chuckle to himself.

The district is dear to the superstitious. Hard by, at the back-gate of Comiston, a belated carter beheld a lady in white, ' with the most beautiful, clear shoes upon her feet,' who looked upon him in a very ghastly manner and then vanished ; and just in front is the Hunters' Tryst, once a roadside inn, and not so long ago haunted by the devil in person. Satan led the inhabitants a pitiful existence. He shook the four corners of the building with lamentable outcries, beat at the doors and windows, overthrew crockery in the dead hours of the morning, and danced unholy dances on the roof. Every kind of spiritual disinfectant was put in requisition ; chosen ministers were summoned out of Edinburgh and prayed by the hour ; pious neighbours sat up all night making a noise of psalmody ; but Satan minded them no more than the wind about the hill-tops ; and it was only after years of persecution, that he left the Hunters' Tryst in peace to occupy himself with the remainder of mankind. What with General Kay, and the white lady, and this singular visitation, the neighbourhood offers great facilities to the makers of sun-myths ; and without exactly casting in one's lot with that disenchanting school of writers, one cannot help hearing a good deal of the winter wind in the last story. ' That nicht,' says Burns, in one of his happiest moments,—

> ' That nicht a child might understand
> The deil had business on his hand.'

And if people sit up all night in lone places on the hills, with Bibles and tremulous psalms, they will be apt to hear some of the most fiendish noises in the world : the wind will beat on doors and dance upon roofs for them, and make the hills howl around their cottage with a clamour like the judgment-day.

The road goes down through another valley, and then finally begins to scale the main slope of the Pentlands A bouquet of old trees stands round a white farmhouse; and from a neighbouring dell, you can see smoke rising and leaves ruffling in the breeze. Straight above, the hills climb a thousand feet into the air. The neighbourhood, about the time of lambs, is clamorous with the bleating of flocks; and you will be awakened, in the grey of early summer mornings, by the barking of a dog or the voice of a shepherd shouting to the echoes. This, with the hamlet lying behind unseen, is Swanston.

The place in the dell is immediately con-

nected with the city. Long ago this sheltered
field was purchased by the Edinburgh magistrates for the sake of the springs that rise or
gather there. After they had built their
water-house and laid their pipes, it occurred
to them that the place was suitable for junket-
ing. Once entertained, with jovial magistrates
and public funds, the idea led speedily to
accomplishment; and Edinburgh could soon
boast of a municipal Pleasure House. The
dell was turned into a garden; and on the
knoll that shelters it from the plain and the
sea winds, they built a cottage looking to the
hills. They brought crockets and gargoyles
from old St. Giles's which they were then
restoring, and disposed them on the gables
and over the door and about the garden ;
and the quarry which had supplied them
with building material, they draped with
clematis and carpeted with beds of roses.
So much for the pleasure of the eye; for
creature comfort, they made a capacious

cellar in the hillside and fitted it with bins
of the hewn stone. In process of time, the
trees grew higher and gave shade to the
cottage, and the evergreens sprang up and
turned the dell into a thicket. There, purple
magistrates relaxed themselves from the pursuit of municipal ambition; cocked hats
paraded soberly about the garden and in
and out among the hollies; authoritative canes
drew ciphering upon the path; and at night,
from high upon the hills, a shepherd saw
lighted windows through the foliage and heard
the voice of city dignitaries raised in song.

The farm is older. It was first a grange of
Whitekirk Abbey, tilled and inhabited by rosy
friars. Thence, after the Reformation, it
passed into the hands of a true-blue Protestant
family. During the covenanting troubles,
when a night conventicle was held upon the
Pentlands, the farm doors stood hospitably
open till the morning; the dresser was laden
with cheese and bannocks, milk and brandy;

and the worshippers kept slipping down from the hill between two exercises, as couples visit the supper-room between two dances of a

Swanston Cottage

modern ball. In the Forty-Five, some foraging Highlanders from Prince Charlie's army fell upon Swanston in the dawn. The great-grandfather of the late farmer was then a little child; him they awakened by plucking the blankets from his bed, and he remembered, when he was an old man, their truculent looks and uncouth speech. The churn stood full of cream in the dairy, and with this they made their brose in high delight. 'It was braw brose,' said one of them. At last, they made off, laden like camels with their booty; and Swanston Farm has lain out of the way of history from that time forward. I do not know what may be yet in store for it. On dark days, when the mist runs low upon the hill, the house has a gloomy air as if suitable for private tragedy. But in hot July, you can fancy nothing more perfect than the garden, laid out in alleys and arbours and bright, old-fashioned flowerpots, and ending in a miniature ravine, all trellis-work and moss and tinkling waterfall, and housed from the sun under fathoms of broad foliage.

The hamlet behind is one of the least considerable of hamlets, and consists of a few

cottages on a green beside a burn. Some of
them (a strange thing in Scotland) are models
of internal neatness; the beds adorned with
patchwork, the shelves arrayed with willow-

EWANSTON
FARM

pattern plates, the floors and tables bright with
scrubbing or pipeclay, and the very kettle
polished like silver. It is the sign of a con-
tented old age in country places, where there
is little matter for gossip and no street sights.
Housework becomes an art; and at evening,

when the cottage interior shines and twinkles
in the glow of the fire, the housewife folds
her hands and contemplates her finished picture; the snow and the wind may do their
worst, she has made herself a pleasant corner
in the world. The city might be a thousand
miles away: and yet it was from close by that
Mr. Bough painted the distant view of Edinburgh which has been engraved for this collec-
tion: and you have only to look at the etching,[*]
to see how near it is at hand. But hills and hill
people are not easily sophisticated; and if you
walk out here on a summer Sunday, it is as
like as not the shepherd may set his dogs upon
you. But keep an unmoved countenance;
they look formidable at the charge, but their
hearts are in the right place; and they will
only bark and sprawl about you on the grass,
unmindful of their master's excitations.

Kirk Yetton forms the north-eastern angle
of the range; thence, the Pentlands trend off

---

[*] Published in the first edition.

to south and west. From the summit you
look over a great expanse of champaign sloping
to the sea and behold a large variety of distant
hills. There are the hills of Fife, the hills of
Peebles, the Lammermoors and the Ochils,
more or less mountainous in outline, more or

The Pentlands

less blue with distance. Of the Pentlands
themselves, you see a field of wild heathery
peaks with a pond gleaming in the midst; and
to that side the view is as desolate as if you
were looking into Galloway or Applecross. To
turn to the other, is like a piece of travel.

O

Far out in the lowlands Edinburgh shows herself, making a great smoke on clear days and spreading her suburbs about her for miles; the Castle rises darkly in the midst; and close by, Arthur's Seat makes a bold figure in the landscape. All around, cultivated fields, and woods, and smoking villages, and white country roads, diversify the uneven surface of the land. Trains crawl slowly abroad upon the railway lines; little ships are tacking in the Firth; the shadow of a mountainous cloud, as large as a parish, travels before the wind; the wind itself ruffles the wood and standing corn, and sends pulses of varying colour across the landscape. So you sit, like Jupiter upon Olympus, and look down from afar upon men's life. The city is as silent as a city of the dead: from all its humming thoroughfares, not a voice, not a footfall, reaches you upon the hill. The sea surf, the cries of ploughmen, the streams and the mill-wheels, the birds and the wind, keep up an animated concert through the plain;

from farm to farm, dogs and crowing cocks contend together in defiance; and yet from this Olympian station, except for the whispering rumour of a train, the world has fallen into a dead silence and the business of town and country grown voiceless in your ears. A crying hill-bird, the bleat of a sheep, a wind singing in the dry grass, seem not so much to interrupt, as to accompany, the stillness ; but to the spiritual ear, the whole scene makes a music at once human and rural, and discourses pleasant reflections on the destiny of man. The spiry habitable city, ships, the divided fields, and browsing herds, and the straight highways, tell visibly of man's active and comfortable ways ; and you may be never so laggard and never so unimpressionable, but there is something in the view that spirits up your blood and puts you in the vein for cheerful labour.

Immediately below is Fairmilehead, a spot of roof and a smoking chimney, where two roads, no thicker than packthread, intersect beside a hanging wood. If you are fanciful, you will be reminded of the gauger in the story. And the thought of this old exciseman, who once lipped and fingered on his pipe and uttered clear notes from it in the mountain air, and the words of the song he affected, carry your mind 'Over the hills and far away' to distant countries ; and you have a vision of Edinburgh not, as you see her, in the midst of a little neighbourhood, but as a boss upon the round world with all Europe and the deep sea for her surroundings. For every place is a centre to the earth, whence highways radiate or ships set sail for foreign ports ; the limit of a parish is not more imaginary than the frontier of an empire ; and as a man sitting at home in his cabinet and swiftly writing books, so a city sends abroad an influence and a portrait of herself. There is no Edinburgh emigrant, far or near, from China to Peru, but he or she carries some lively pictures of the mind, some sunset behind the Castle cliffs, some snow scene, some maze of city lamps, indelible in the memory and delightful to study in the intervals of toil. For any such, if this book fall in their way, here are a few more home pictures. It would be pleasant, if they should recognise a house where they had dwelt, or a walk that they had taken.

THE END

RICHARD CLAY AND SONS, LIMITED, LONDON AND BUNGAY

THE SPECTATOR IN LONDON.

Essays by ADDISON and STEELE. With more than 100 Illustrations by RALPH CLEAVER and other artists. Crown 8vo, in handsome binding, gilt edges, 6s.

"A glance at the table of contents will give most of us a new conception of the comprehensiveness of the humour of the two great essayists. London lodgings, London signs, and London cries ; the lives of the coffee-houses ; the performances at the opera and play-house ; the numberless whims of fashionable life, and of the life which ministers to fashions, all have their place. . . The comedy of the situations is excellently caught by Mr. Cleaver, who likewise supplies us with an inexhaustible variety of pretty faces."—*Guardian.*

"His drawings show a lively power of imagination, a sufficient sense of humour, and a thorough sympathy with his author."—*Scotsman.*

"A prettily illustrated book."—*Daily News.*

"There are many illustrations in the volume, and most of them interpret cleverly the manners, the dress, the leisure of a former phase of society, so that in black and white, with pen and pencil, the old times live again."—*Leeds Mercury.*

"The selection of papers has been very judiciously made, and the beautiful illustrations from the pencil of Mr. Ralph Cleaver give a new vividness even to the descriptions by Mr. Spectator's pen."—*Glasgow Herald.*

"It is superfluous to speak well of these papers. But here they are in the prettiest of editions, fully illustrated by Mr. Cleaver, who has a graceful, dainty, and humorous pencil. Presented so, the essays will easily oust for a quiet hour any of the books of our own day."—*Bookman.*

"A most enticing selection of our favourite Addison and Steele morsels, with pen and ink drawings by Mr. Ralph Cleaver, in which that artist has excellently well caught the eighteenth century air."—*Queen.*

BY THE AUTHOR OF "OUR VILLAGE."

COUNTRY STORIES. By MARY

RUSSELL MITFORD. With 70 Illustrations by GEORGE MORROW. Crown 8vo, in handsome binding, with gilt edges, 6s.

"A beautiful edition, with illustrations by Mr. George Morrow that are actually worthy of the text, of Mary Russell Mitford's delicious 'Country Stories.'"—*Spectator.*

"The book is well got up and very prettily bound, and Mr. Morrow's pictures are clever, quaint, and amusing. It will make a charming gift book, and it cannot be too widely circulated."—*Scotsman.*

"We can well understand the popularity of Miss Mitford's stories. They are very well written, and full of little touches which could only have been given by one who lived in the country and loved it."—*Athenæum.*

"We do not now have such tales written for us as Miss Mitford's 'Country Stories.' They are like the gossip and cowslip wine genially dispensed by some placid old ladies we ave known, whose hospitality was always reached through rose-covered porches."—*Sketch.*

SEELEY AND CO., LIMITED, Essex Street, Strand.